HANDCUFFED EMOTIONS

'A POLICE INTERCEPTOR'S DRIVE INTO DARKNESS'

BENJAMIN PEARSON

With

PATRICIA SUTCLIFFE

DEDICATION

I dedicate this book to:

Leyton, Milly, Harriet, and Isaac

'Thank you for being the brightest stars on the

darkest nights'

ACKNOWLEDGEMENTS

Patricia Sutcliffe

for helping make this possible

Sgt Lyon, Sgt Lund, PC 576 'Shabba' Taylor & PC 4791 Alam

for their support and friendship

Therapist Paul Buckley

for his healing words

Jonathan Crabtree

for his excellent cover design

James Warner

for his photography

To my family and friends who care enough to understand

FOREWORD

To talk openly about Post Traumatic Stress Disorder (PTSD) takes courage and strength, In Benjamin Pearson's memoir **'Handcuffed Emotions - A Police Interceptor's drive into darkness'.** Both are in abundance. It's a hard-hitting, honest account of what it's like to live with an unseen menace that robs its victims of everything they hold close. PTSD disturbs thoughts, feelings, and dreams, altering how a person reacts to situations, twisting reality, changing behaviour, robbing the sufferer of rational thought, leaving them tormented.

Benjamin Pearson is a highly trained 'police interceptor' with 19 years' experience in the force. He has undertaken intensive instruction to gain the skills needed to face the daily traumas of his role. Ben has also achieved celebrity status as one of the traffic cops featured in Channel 5's 'Police Interceptors' 'reality' programme that has enhanced the persona of an elite traffic cop, making them recognisable.   What isn't revealed is the internal struggle the role carries with it. In 'Handcuffed Emotions' Ben exposes the truth about PTSD and the battle he faces daily.

Sadness, borne out of despair becomes more poignant because of its similarity to the experiences of those in similar jobs, highlighted in the 2018 survey, 'The Job & The Life' examined trauma resilience in UK Policing. It exposed the suffering of over 18000 officers and staff and revealed the shocking statistic that 1 in 5 reported symptoms of PTSD or Complex PTSD, five times higher than in the UK population.

The torment faced by Ben is told in his own voice, the events real, and the aftermath, life changing. His memories of the incidents leading to diagnosis are as vivid as they are mentally destructive. 'Handcuffed Emotions' cannot help but make the reader grieve at the lack of support offered to Ben from the establishment.

X

The traumatic events are too many to re-count. Incidents involving child fatalities, human limbs de-gloved, and cars cut in two on impact. Ben re-tells the impact of such violent tragedies with honesty and accuracy. He relives his 19 years on the force in vivid detail from his days as a trainee and commended officer through to the enveloping darkness of PTSD.

This book is a gripping tale of reality and bravery. It examines the struggles that police officers' face in the daily battle against the criminal element of our society. Laying bare the life-changing decisions that keep the evil from the doors of the public. Decisions that safeguard each of us. Protecting us from the unseen darkness that lurks, allowing us to sleep, safe, in our beds at night.

Benjamin Pearson, in writing such an authentic account of his life, aims to heighten public perception of 'the role behind the badge.' What it means and to help change the way employers deal with PTSD in the workplace.

'I felt numb and disconnected, something was wrong with me and I knew it'

In the Beginning–A Pivotal Decision

I was born in 1976 and as a 70s child, addicted to the classic 80s cop shows. My mind developed with the likes of TJ Hooker, Dempsey & Makepeace, and the Professionals. My favourite by far was ChiPs. A series about the California Highway Patrol. I relished the action, car chases and fights. The opening scene I remember clearly to this day. My hero Frank Poncherello and his sidekick, Jon Barker riding side by side onto the Californian freeway to the sound of cheesy 70s music that boasted an epic baseline and rifting guitar. How I admired those boys little did I know, how the reality of the show would pan out in my own life.

My dream began when I was still an impressionable seventeen-year-old. I remember it well; The day had started normally enough, just as any other day, but ended in an incident that literally changed my life. I was on my way home when I saw a shop that was ablaze; a man lay trapped behind the door. Half of the small corner shop had collapsed; fire was raging through its only window. I desperately wanted to help. My instincts were to go in there and get him out. Save him. The police and fire brigade hadn't arrived, so I went in with another passer-by to drag the man out. My black leather jacket was covered in dark soot and my left knuckles were burnt. I remember being surprised and thinking something wasn't right when the male fled from the scene without so much as a thank you. It turned out it was the shopkeeper who was the arsonist; he had tried to burn down his own premises as an insurance scam and risked losing his life to do it. That was the day I lost my innocence in human nature.

HANDCUFFED EMOTIONS

My realisation that there were 'Two Worlds' out there and that the safe one I lived in ran alongside a much darker, twisted one began the start of an obsession. I began watching every 'real' crime programme I could, taking a powerful interest in the way criminals worked. The more I absorbed, the more my interest in human nature grew. I became fascinated with the work of the police and I wanted to be part of it. Cliché as it sounds, I wanted to help the good guys. I wanted to be one of the good guys; I didn't want to go on a power trip or be a hero. I just wanted to make a difference. Perhaps it related back to those 80s cop shows, who knows? I just knew I wanted to give something back to society.

At the time I worked selling motorcycles, a love of mine, something I still enjoy doing. I didn't realise at the time that working with bikes would bring about the realisation of my dream. Bobbies enjoy bikes so there was always a few coming into the shop and I got to know them. I admired the lives they led, the adrenaline and energy they seemed to possess. My life was dull in comparison. I had an amazing boss, worked for a brilliant company, but something was missing. Sadly, I was also very insecure as a person. I lacked confidence to put myself forward. How could someone like me, with dyslexia, hope to join the police force? I hadn't done particularly well at school; I didn't see myself as intelligent. I was just a regular, likeable lad who enjoys a drink with his mates.

Amazingly, the coppers who visited the shop saw something different in me, so with their encouragement and a lot of false courage, I applied to become a police officer. I sent off my application expecting to hear nothing. So was shocked to find myself accepted for an interview. I recall my stomach doing somersaults. I had a chance. A small one, but a chance and I would take it. I would give it my all.

The idea of two days of tests followed by an interview, that could change my life, filled me with trepidation. Clothed in my brother's best suit that hung on my slim frame, I entered the room. 'Take your jacket off lad' commanded the officer. 'I'm all right, thank you.' My reply was hesitant and covering the truth. What I really meant was 'I can't sir. Fear and perspiration have wet my shirt through, and my nipples are showing'. What I was doing there at all, God only knew.

The first test began. Called the carousel, it involved role play and decision-making scenarios that I somehow struggled my

4

way through. I remember the locked rooms. There was a piece of A4 on the door describing the incident. '*You are a security guard at Arndale Shopping Centre, Luke is 5 years old and is missing. His mother is waiting for you. You have 30 seconds to read the brief and then 10 minutes in the room.*' You cannot finish early or late and there is an independent person watching and marking what you say. The pressure is on you from the minute you read the brief.

Next came the physical and finally the interview day. It felt intense, although meant to be relaxed. I learned that they designed the questions to see how many blue cubes you had or needed to be a good copper. Police speak for characteristics. Apparently, I had half a body full. It's like building blocks. The more you have, the more you are complete as a full-blooded bobby with the right attitudes and personality traits. If you can imagine blue blocks slotting into place, with each new block you lose a bit of who you are and become more of the force. Then they explained the 'Wave' analogy. I was told that if I thought I would make a difference, to think again. I was told squarely that I would never make a difference, but that I was part of the wall of society. The blue line that separated good from bad. Once I stepped out of that line, they would replace me. It was that simple. It would take me 19 years to realise it was also that true.

As a fit lad, I returned home, confident I had passed the physical but doubtful of little else. The following days dragged as memories of the interview sank into oblivion. Then, after what seemed an eternity, an envelope dropped through the letter box. Tentatively, I picked it up. I could see through the address box window the police logo above my name. Telling myself it was a rejection letter, I opened it. The word 'congratulations' sprang out of the page. To say it stunned me is an understatement. It was there in black and white. I was to report on the 1st October 2001 at Bishopgarth, Wakefield, where I would remain for two weeks.

In the weeks before my journey began, the days seemed to slow down. Then, bang, it was here. I arrived at the gates. I carried one small bag for the week. 'Bring the minimum' the letter had said. I did just that. It didn't take me long to realise that I was ill prepared with the paltry amount of clothing I had brought with me. Walking around in the same trousers, shirt and tie all day long and into the evenings became more than embarrassing. In my naivety, I thought they would issue me with my uniform when I arrived.

I remember as I walked through the car park I felt so alone. Goodbyes, good lucks, kisses, and hugs surrounded me as parents and friends said farewell to their loved ones. I had no one to say goodbye to me. Several of the new recruits were teary; I tried to be macho. Inside I was shit scared, but I would not show it. The realisation that I was a little fish in a big pond and out of my depth hit me all too quickly. My thoughts were everywhere, and I was rapidly becoming overwhelmed at the challenge I knew lay ahead.

I entered a large hall full of scared, would be coppers. A sea of unknown faces all around. Then I looked to my left side, my heart leapt, I recognised the face of a lad that had lived opposite me. Dave was his name, and the relief was instantaneous. Then I spotted another that I knew. It was a great friend of mine named Leigh. I settled down. We were to remain together for the next 17 weeks.

BENJAMIN PEARSON

The two weeks at Bishopgarth went by in a flash. If I thought I knew about life and how the World works, I was in for one hell of a shock. I knew nothing. So, I pretended to be tougher and wiser than I was, but I didn't have a clue. Even though I learnt quickly, I struggled; I felt that I was trying twice as hard for half as much. Determination was on my side, however, and I tackled every task with all I had. I would be someone who I wanted to be, or at least who I thought I wanted to be.

I learned to use computers; I'd never used one before. Mastered drills whilst being nose to nose with a screaming drill sergeant. I wanted to laugh. It was all bravado to cover the fear I really felt. I learned about unarmed combat and handcuffing techniques, yes there are techniques to arresting a person. They taught me how to march. I felt like I was in prison, but I was learning how to be a copper and an excellent one. I saw recruits who had done something stupid or broken the law disappear from the training camp. It made me all the keener to get through my time and feel the weight of my uniform on my body for the first time. Be part of the team. An important element of training. I was to learn later that you are part of a team but one that is owned by the West Yorkshire Police.

HANDCUFFED EMOTIONS

During the day, as recruits we worked hard to prove ourselves, during the night we proved ourselves differently. We would go into the town for a drink, but we knew that if we went into nightclubs, we had to leave our names so they would know where we had been. It was a common to put down the name of trainers, so it appeared they had been on the booze in every nightclub in the town. I used to put the Chief Constables name down with a smiley face next to it. 'Be discreet' we were told. 'Don't draw any attention to yourselves.' Funny how a few beers quickly erase all common sense and memory. It only took a few quick pints for us to run to the front of a nightclub queue, flash our warrant cards and shout. 'Let me in, I'm the law.' Worked every time to the knowing laughter of the door staff. I won't go into detail about the activities in the corridors at night sufficient to say, many of us continued to prove ourselves there as well.

Ironically, we were all paranoid and suspected that they had secret camera's around the place to keep track of our activities. We also thought they had enticed us to go out at the weekends just so they could catch us up to mischief. I have to be honest and say the first two weeks at Bishopgarth and the last two weeks at Bishopgarth in 2001 were like been on an 18-30's holiday. Respectable in the daytime, but all hell let loose at night. Boys became men in many ways. I know it's all changed now, but that was then, and we were residential so didn't have to drive anywhere.

All measurements taken; the day came to collect my uniform. It was a magic moment; I felt like a child again as they showed me how to dress, even down to the way to put on my helmet. Funny as that sounds, the host of attachments on a police uniform takes some getting used to. They must fit in the right place, be accessible and easily available if needed. Not so simple to do correctly without training, training I became grateful for.

I vividly remember the self-assuredness I felt the day I put that uniform on. I had gone through two weeks of hell, being screamed at, watched, and assessed at every step, but now, plain Benjamin Pearson was somebody. I hoped I would be a force to be reckoned with. I had changed. The instant I put my uniform on, I allowed my alter ego to take over. The highlight receiving my collar number '1965'. A number I am still proud of even today.

HANDCUFFED EMOTIONS

If I thought the working days at Bishopgarth were hard, the 17 weeks I spent at Ashford Police Training Centre opened my eyes to what being a police officer really meant. I remember when we first arrived at Ashford. We were little fish in an even bigger pond. There were these huge dorms. You had to stand outside and wait for them to call your number. They shouted about four of us together and one was a lad called Adam, another from Yorkshire. We walked into this corridor with about 50 rooms and we were the last two rooms. I was once again with strangers but one thing that made my life brilliant during my training was the different people; I met from all over the country. People I still call my friends today.

The corridor was full of Essex, Sussex and the Met, walking around with bare chests and towels around their waists. Then we heard a voice in a strong Essex accent say, 'Hello mate'. We replied, 'Now then'. To a chorus of 'Northerners, fucking hell, northerners.' We told them we were from Bradford in West Yorkshire. It chuffed them, they felt they had their drinking partners in us. Then Adam, quick off the mark, chirped out, 'Yeh but we don't drink lager tops.' An array of jovial boos followed.

BENJAMIN PEARSON

Getting back to Wakefield for the final two weeks was exciting. I had walked in lacking confidence and scared. I would walk out a bone fide 'Protector of the People'. Secure in my abilities. My parents were living in Spain at the time so I hadn't seen them in a while and couldn't wait to greet them at the gates on pass out day. There I stood smiling, bursting with pride then laughing as they walked straight past me. I was unrecognisable amongst all the other blue uniforms.

The glow on their faces. It's something I will never forget. Then came the tears of joy. Seeing my dad cry was something I had never experienced before; he was a down-to-earth Yorkshire man and Yorkshire men don't cry. I was no longer Ben who tries hard; I was Ben who succeeds. Ben, the Police Officer, respected and thanked as a protector of the public. It didn't take me long to realise I was only at the beginning of what would become a long and hard, learning curve.

My first step onto the steep learning ladder came early, very early. They warned us not to go home in uniform because at that stage of our careers we really didn't know what to do if anyone attacked us. As an officer, I could be a target. Now telling someone who is bursting with power, even a power they do not understand how to use, what is the first thing they do? Well for me, I drove straight to my brother's house in full uniform with my belt on. I stood outside like a peacock preening, waiting for him and everyone else to see me. My ego had taken over, I wanted to scream from the rooftops, 'Hey I'm a Policeman'. Then it dawned, slowly but surely. If someone comes up to me asking for help or were being attacked, I will shit myself.

BENJAMIN PEARSON

Forget Planet Sandford

I was now part of a team, a brother, and sisterhood of people who would always have my back and never let me down. I could rely on them and they could rely on me. We were family. I was still young and still naïve. I was also full of life and mine was about to begin. Unless you've worn a service uniform whether it be Police, Ambulance, Fire service or Armed forces. It's hard to understand the feelings you have that first day on the job. The excitement in your stomach mixed with anticipation. Questioning yourself. Are you ready to serve the public? Noticing how your friends now treat you with more respect. Admire your achievement.

15

There is a weird feeling of belonging. You are with people who would die for you and you would die for them. Your uniform, irrespective of what force you belonged to, is your badge of honour. You became one massive family immediately after you put it on. Brothers and sisters to the end. I've never experienced such a bond. It felt amazing. You would go on operations where police from all over the country would merge. The difference armed forces would look at each other, checking you out. Taking the piss out of each other. You didn't really talk to each other, but if you met each other over a bar in Majorca and asked what each other did, you would be instantly best mates

You know that out of 1000 that may have applied to become a police officer, only 250 got interviewed, only 100 made it through to the carousel. For the paper sift only 52 made it and you are one of them. It fills you with an incredible self-belief and pride. Now, you are ready to do anything required of you. You have achieved what others couldn't and you now possess a selection of 'toys' so you can do your job and you must prove you know how to use them.

HANDCUFFED EMOTIONS

The term, 'Live and Breathe the Job' becomes reality. You feel an immense responsibility to those you have pledged to help. To your Crown and Country. My first weeks went by in a haze that cleared little by little, opening my eyes to an unfamiliar existence and one I hadn't known before. I saw and experienced things that no training school or television programme had prepared me for. I was now working on the black side of life. A side that law-abiding citizens know little about or want to.

During my first ten weeks on the job, I was a 'proby' (probationer) and assigned a tutor. Although not much older than me, she was an experienced officer who introduced me to the 'real' job. The first thing she taught me was to forget what I had learned in training school because it meant nothing out in the actual World. That turned out to be an understatement!

My first posting as a beat bobby was in Keighley, made up of urban, rural and two competing gangs. The Top Enders and the Bottom Enders. It just so happened on the day before I started. Amidst a background of drug dealing, a 24-year-old male had been murdered in the middle of the afternoon. The attack, nothing short of horrific. The victim had an axe imbedded at the back of his head before being stabbed. All hell had let loose and a gang war was looming. This was the environment I stepped into as a new bobby.

I learned quickly that the saying 'There is no honour amongst thieves,' is true. This code of silence they talk about is rubbish. You will always get one that sings like a canary. Honour goes out of the window. There is a real lack of structure to the way criminals lead their lives, to the way we lead ours. Christmas Day doesn't exist because they are out committing burglaries. They think nothing of stealing from a church. It's their normality. Literally, if someone had a heart attack and fell on the floor, the first thing they would do is empty their pockets. The lack of caring is astounding. They could see someone run over and have their brains stuck on their feet. They will laugh, waiting for it to be on You Tube. This was a steep learning curve for me. It wasn't a humanity I knew or understood.

I was always ready for action; I was just the proby who made tea with his stab vest on and gloves tucked in my belt, just in case. This sounds normal today, but in 2001 nobody wore stab vests until they absolutely had to. Back then they were made from slabs of wood and concrete and spent most of their lives in the boot of a patrol car. Today the vests are vastly different and wearing them is compulsory.

Over the next months, my moral compass changed. Every day opened my eyes to things I never knew existed. I realised how much my upbringing had sheltered me. Although my background was working class, there had always been food on the table. My father had worked his fingers to the bone to provide for us. It wasn't caviar and champagne, but there was always a good solid meal on the table.

Now I was seeing a face of society I knew little about. Visiting houses that were filthy, kids with dirty nappies, days old. Needles strewn around the floor where they played. Dog shit and cat piss on the carpets. Occupiers who had no respect for themselves or anyone else. These were the people who just didn't care or had long since given up. I was dealing with hardened criminals daily, shoplifters who stole for drugs and those who stole out of a need to eat. Rightly or wrongly, I felt the latter to be more acceptable. The saddest cases.

BENJAMIN PEARSON

It was a wintry afternoon when I got called to one such case. A supermarket whose 'no tolerance' policy they keenly enforced. I entered the security office to see a scared 85-year-old lady, visibly shaking. Her crime, she had stolen a packet of Hobnobs. Normally, as a young officer you follow the rules blindly, but now I quickly learned the value of making sensible judgements. Having subjected myself to a series of moral questions, I refused to arrest her. An annoyed manager threatened to report me, I gave him permission. He didn't, and they took no further action. Sometimes you must use plain common sense in deciding what action to take.

As a police officer, you develop a 6th sense that puts you on alert when assessing situations. You know when something is wrong, or someone is lying to you. Your bullshit-ohmmeter goes stratospheric. You sense when a call out is about to turn violent. There are many times when I have been called out to a domestic. I have arrived with my partner at some back to back terraced house to find a male kicking off with his wife. Adrenaline pumping, I move in to stop the fight only for the male to lunge straight at me. At the time that happens, you go numb and think of nothing other than getting the situation under control. It is only back at the station that you realise you have been injured in the fracas.

Some incidents they have called me out to are almost farcical if it wasn't for the seriousness of them. One, I remember well, happened during my first days as a copper. I faced a man stood in a kitchen threatening his wife. He was around 5'4" wearing nothing but his wife's fluffy green dressing gown. Now at 6'2" I'm a big lad, so felt no threat at all until he went for my female partner with a knife. She immediately sprayed him with CS gas that covered us both, making it hard to breathe. I still had to stop him, so I made a grab for him to find as little as he was, he was strong. We ended up grappling on the floor with his private parts dangling in my face and few options left that I could grab hold of. I think twice now when I'm called 'dickhead' by some young yobbo playing the tough guy in front of his mates.

For all the awful stuff, there is also a lot of quality stuff. I learned the importance of remaining non-judgemental from Sam, my first partner. She epitomised the phrase 'without fear or favour', basing her decisions on hard evidence. Sam had experience in dealing with rape cases and emphasised to me the need to look at the 'outer' scene and the 'inner' scene. For example. She taught me the importance of inspecting the entire scene and ask questions before we make an arrest; Who let the man in? Was he invited in? How did he get into the bedroom? Are there signs of forced entry? Has a struggle taken place?

It was when I was with Sam attending a domestic; I had my first violent encounter. I got hit on the head trying to reason with the occupier. It would be the first of many. No day is the same when you're a police officer. What remains the same is the cloak of resilience you put on with your uniform. The image you are in complete control, all personal feelings set aside. I realised too late; the actual power of the emotions you keep hidden deep inside on your sanity.

Sometimes the day becomes lightened by some bizarre incident you couldn't write if you tried. Like the time there had been a jewellery burglary, and we chased down the criminal in the middle of the town centre. I was trying to get hold of him, and he was running around a car with me trying to get him on the other side. It must have looked like a scene out of the keystone cops to onlookers, with stolen goods dropping from his coat and hidden down his two pair of pants. Finally, I jumped over the bonnet and tackled him, Jewellery scattered all over the place, but I cuffed him to the applause of the bystanders and beeping car horns. A pleasant change from being spat on by them.

We also have the 'love the uniform' women who are remarkably diverse, from your 17-year-old up to 99-year-old. The sexual innuendo's they throw out can be unbelievable. They have often asked me to handcuff them for the pure thrill. Comments like 'have you got a big helmet' and 'show me your big baton' or 'does your baton extend' are commonplace. I take it all in a day's work.

When you are a beat officer, you expect to be dragged from pillar to post, day in, day out. The dedication given to the job is unreal. It's not something you question; you just get on with it; just work hard and have a thirst to help. Beat bobbies deserve a lot more credit than what they get. They place beat officers in every situation, some of which they are ill prepared for. Assaults, domestics, street fights, but your day still isn't over.

BENJAMIN PEARSON

You're in the station, winding down, looking at that day's injured colleagues, and there are always some officers injured. Clothing ripped, bloodied knees, gashes.

As a beat officer, you are the first contact for the community. You were on foot when I joined and covered your area. It was all about interacting with the public and reassuring them. Your beat is a territory and a time in police terminology. It's the job where you learn first-hand what policing is about. It's a constant learning environment where you are called upon to deal with anything from a stolen bike to a group of piss heads wanting a fight. I would say, without doubt, that as a beat cop you are the backbone of the force.

It can, however, be a thankless role where it's common to feel undervalued and overlooked. Working out on the streets, it's the beat officer that most of the public will meet. The person who they will turn to when in need and who they expect to help them. It's also the person in the firing line for abuse and violence. When you go out on the beat, you are constantly taking a risk, making decisions that may not fit in with what the public think should happen but every police officer is ruled by polices, regulations and procedures that cover every facet of the work we do. One misjudgement can land you with a suspension and an in-depth investigation into your actions…'grabbing the brass rail' as it's known to officers. Few other jobs have such pressures placed upon them. It can leave you in a no-win situation, and that causes immense stress and self-retribution.

Injuries are commonplace, we know and expect them. What we find hard to accept is that the perpetrators who may end up in prison see it as a training ground. They come out far savvier than when they went in. Television keeps them fully in touch with the outside. Free meals and a fully equipped gym keep them strong and healthy. Then out they come, their skills honed. You will hear them refer to Prison as a holiday camp. These are the reprobates who will walk over your body to escape. I've had to deal with murderers, rapist and kiddie touchers caught on CCTV, but they will still look you in the face and lie. They will even swear on the Bible or Quran dependent upon whatever religion and not care a toss.

In my early years as a cop, stealing cars was all about 'joy riding'. Now, it's about taking cars to do armed robberies or sell them on to order. Everything's done digitally. They know how to start cars from driveways without the keys. Most are aware of forensics because it's all on the net. They prime their mobile phones with data on houses, what time they leave for work. Type of car they have, what time they will return. Trackers are used and placed beneath cars, so they know where people are. They will follow you home and observe your house. There is intelligence in what they do. If they put as much effort into normal work, they would do well in life.

Everything has graded up. Using technology has improved our ability to track down criminals, but it's also assisted criminals in evading police. Scanners, tracker blockers in cigarette lighters. These are all the little toys they use to commit crime. The villains of today are a far cry from those depicted in programme's like Dixon of Dock Green or the Krays. They are sophisticated and dangerous. The crews that are running around, dealing drugs, and committing robberies are getting younger every day. They recruit school kids to do their selling using throw away phones. If they get caught, there is no link back. The car will be from a hire company. Their carrier will be someone with no criminal history to drive it from A to B. When questioned, they know nothing.

HANDCUFFED EMOTIONS

Drugs are big money-makers for dealers and the networks they set up, ingenious. They have pyramid systems whereby the bottom rung comprises the drug takers. The runners, as we know them, who get paid in fixes. They live their miserable lives distributing drugs for a drug. That's it. Living in such a world is all they know. A pathetic existence, but it's what they choose. The lowest of the low are those at the top of the triangle. Money rakes who live the high life on the backs of the addicts. Often, they are selling watered down drugs laden with rat poison, salt, anything that makes it cheaper to produce, they add. The price has come down drastically, so the quantity must be more to make the same profit. I can catch runners with 100 wraps on them and that can carry a prison sentence of up with 4 years.

Billy Jo Scroat, drug boss, couldn't care less. Runners are easy come, easy go. Even the runners have runners known as non-entities, in that nothing is known about them. You stop the rental car; It goes like this; 'Who are you? 'I don't know'. 'Where are you?' same reply. He has no chalks against him, so we can't connect him to anything. We know they are runners crossing county lines. Recruiting kids to do the work for them.

They could have 4kgs of heroin in their cars worth hundreds of thousands of pounds, which they deny any knowledge of.

I go shopping and I wear a baseball cap when I'm in my civvies. Why? I must cover up my white streak because I'm easily known by it in the same way I know the criminals who might stand in the queue behind me. Being in the police taints the way you look at things and people. You can look at the cereal choices on the shelf. Whilst doing so, I am aware of who is around me and what they are up to. My white streak that I keep mentioning is caused by a genetic condition called 'Waardenburg's Syndrome'. It's a rare condition resulting in a white forelock that makes me instantly recognisable.

Things have changed now with beat bobbies. The days of walking your patch on foot are long gone, now it's an area you drive around. I can say that beat bobbies today miss so much by not walking the streets. I loved it; you couldn't walk more than a few feet without someone offering you a brew. You got to know shop keepers and residents alike. The job was different; you were walking miles and miles a day, and it was brilliant. You learned more talking to people than ever you would sitting in your car.

HANDCUFFED EMOTIONS

Having a car also had its advantages. As a young cop I remember one day when I was driving along, and I passed two nice looking girls who appeared lost. I slowed down and stopped and asked them how they were doing and if they needed any help. They told me they didn't need my help but thanked me for asking.

Smug in my police uniform and feeling that I was the man, I put the car into reverse and backed straight into a wall. What a Pratt I felt. I did hope the girls I was trying to help, hadn't seen that I had backed into a wall. The look on their faces told me different.

I smile now when I look back at those days, but I was young. My ego was raging, and I felt I was invincible. Now I know that I am not invincible, no one is.

My days on the beat taught me so much about policing. I also learned how to deal with people in a correct manner. I found that if you give respect, you will get respect from the public in general. This of course changes with the criminal element who respect no one, not even themselves.

BENJAMIN PEARSON

I'll Leave it with Ya Kid

In my first four and a half years in the force, I worked as a 'beat' officer, learning the trade, you could say, getting some wool on my back. I then became a tutor constable, training rookies before moving to the drugs team for a brief spell. All the while I'm building up my skills, gaining experience. more of those blue blocks are slotting into place.

The one job that always sticks out in my mind was when I did a stint on the drugs team and we did a drug raid on a house. Now when you are doing a drug raid, you must tear the place apart. We leave no stone unturned. We set to work, but the house appeared to be clean of drugs. Then we got a call through to tell us we were in number 6 when we should be at number 8, next door. Shit! We'd bust the wrong house.

Next came the move that was to change my life big time. I applied for and got accepted to join the special ops department as a traffic cop. Known in the force as an RPU cop, seen as a black rat. 'Would do their own grandmothers given the chance.' I used to hear. I was 28 years of age, still eager and young enough to make a difference. It was the job I believed I was born to do but hadn't realised. I was back to my need to help others, my compassion, strong and real.

I knew it was a dangerous job, one of the most dangerous in the force. I would deal with desperate criminals who cared for nothing but getting away. I knew there would be those who wouldn't think twice of ramming my traffic car and killing me. Their only concern to outfox and out drive the advanced drivers. Escape at all costs. It was kudos for them.

The training was intense, building up my expertise bit by bit, job by job. I became an advanced driver, trained in TPAC (Tactical Pursuit and Containment) and tactical contact on stolen vehicles. I was one of the elites. Risking life and limb with every pursuit in the line of duty. I was in the job that all boy racers think they will love. The thought of racing around in a fast car, catching baddies, eating drive throughs, and getting paid loads of cash. The Starkey and Hutch image. They do not understand the reality at all.

I had a great tutor when I joined traffic, now a lifelong friend. John was one of the old school traffic cops. He was the shiny shoe, crisp shirt and tie man carrying an old document folder briefcase. One of the first things he said when he met me was. 'Listen carefully. You now get paid for what you know and the skills you have, so remember this phrase.' I waited expectantly for this glint of secret knowledge. He peered at me with a serious face and remarked. 'I'll leave it with ya kid.' He explained that traffic officers hardly get their pens out other than to write a ticket or prosecute someone. Unless there is a car involved or motor vehicle, you leave them to it. It may have been light-hearted old school banter, but John taught me so much. How to be firm but fair, to be professional always. I will be grateful for his teachings to the end of my days.

Imagine driving at 110-mph in a 30-mph limit. A stolen car in front of you. Members of the public to either side, people walking on the kerb. In the rear-view mirror three other pursuit vehicles with lights and sirens distracting you, five feet from your rear end. You're watching the road layout and the view ahead. You are giving commentary and exact location in a calm, controlled voice. Listening to the reply's, planning a place in your head. You must also remember road traffic law and work with your knowledge of the area. You are moving at 161 feet per second. The ability to drive and multitask at the same time takes an incredible amount of energy and concentration. It focuses your senses on the scene. You and your car are the same. You become meshed together. There is a numbness. A man in a machine. You feel nothing; it becomes automatic, locked in time.

BENJAMIN PEARSON

You are asking yourself the questions. Where is the helicopter? Are there ambulances on scene? Watch for the car coming out of the roadside. Will there be fatalities? It goes on and on and you must know the answers. There is no time to hesitate at all. Then, there is the aftermath, your hands are shaking, adrenaline charging. In an instant, there's a high you go through that comes down quickly. You cannot focus, then you have the debrief. You think of the consequences and reflect. Self-analysis takes over. Back in the office, full of alpha males and females, you joke and laugh to relieve the stress, but it's still there. You get home and only then, when you are alone, does the deep thinking begin.

I learned quickly that the reality of a day as a Police Interceptor is like no other. On an early shift I get up at 5.45am, shave, have a bit of breakfast and get off to work. I'm at work for 6.20 and it starts. I get my kit bag, a critical accessory that holds everything needed to do my job. It could be a hammer, rope, gloves, screwdriver. The things I know I will need from experience on the job. I check I have my CS gas and radio. By 7.00 am I am officially on duty. I have a de-brief of the events of the evening before, I'm told what's outstanding and then I am out in my car ready and prepared to fight crime.

HANDCUFFED EMOTIONS

My normal area is Bradford or Airedale, it's a vast area stretching from Keighley up to Skipton, Shipley, Otley, etc. Much of it is urban roads, so fast roads, a lot of fatalities. Also, a lot of crime with the richer areas of Leeds on one side, Harrogate down the road and North Yorkshire. It means that criminals must go through your patch and back from where they are committing activity. It makes it a good ground to work to catch the burgling shits.

I am also aware from the brief; what cars they have stolen the night before. We might do a reckie of the shitty estates to see where they have dumped them or if they are still using them, which then means we are in for a pursuit. If nothing is coming in on the radio, we go about our normal tasks. For example, someone had knocked a kid down outside a school. Parents are up in arms so we will police the area and give a ticket to anyone parked illegally. It's important to reassure the public and let them see we are doing our job.

This is the start of the day. As the day goes on and the roads get busier, the bump calls start coming in with reports of injuries, some slight, others fatal. Then it gets to 11am and the crime element has woken up. Billy the Shit needs his fix, so the dealers come out, no license, no insurance, and a car full of drugs. By that time, you might have five or six different reports coming in and you are trying to deal with them all whilst keeping alert to everything around you. They drag you in in many directions.

All the time your 'copper's nose' is kicking in. You know by experience what will be happening. You know the area you need to be in, then you must decide. Do I sit here and wait for a car to come through or go find it? What's the best option, my best chance to catch a driver of a stolen car or prevent some fatality occurring? Your adrenaline plateaus, but your senses are heightening. You know if something will happen or not. Your hands get cold. Then, bump you're on, there has been an armed robbery. Another car is radioing that the criminal's car is on its way to you. Your adrenaline starts up, you can hear the car coming, its engine revving. Sirens screaming. You get a stinger in place, you have just one chance. As the car comes towards you at 100 miles an hour you feel the wind in your hair with the force. The smell of the fuel gets in your nostrils, bits of grit hit you in the face. If you have successfully stung the tyre of the speeding car, you feel elated. Within seconds it's over. They have boxed the car in. Your only concern now. Is anyone injured? Is the scene secured? You know that the occupants of the stolen car don't give a shit for anything apart from getting away.

This is every day, and it's nothing like that shown on television. We are on normal roads meant traffic travelling at 30/40 miles an hour; chasing a car reaching speeds of over 100mph with other vehicles on the road. Then we stop the suspects, who have choices, get out and fight or put their hands up. You don't know which, but we must be ready. Once we have them in cuffs, we are spat at, kicked, and called a piggy bastard. We get abuse, but we must look after them, respect them, give them their rights. It can end in minutes, but then comes six hours or more paperwork. It can deflate, I must record every detail. Body cam footage, all evidence collected. Only then do I go home to my partner so she can go to work on the night shift. It can be so exhausting, especially if, like me, you consider you are a good cop. One who goes out looking for the dangerous guys and protecting the public. Someone who is accountable.

The red tape is frustrating. As a bobby I want to be out catching the criminals, not completing hours and hours of paperwork. I am lucky if I get a mealtime, then I come in for more abuse and get reported. Somebody saw me in ASDA carpark grabbing a sandwich and questions why I am I not doing my work. I've attending a fatal road accident where somebody has brought me a cup of tea for someone else to shout. 'Haven't you got anything fucking better to do. Go get a proper job.' There I stand; a fatal scene in front of me, a body being removed. I've been on duty 10 hours without a drink and I'm suddenly classed as unprofessional.

The amount of skill needed to do your job if you are a traffic cop is unchallengeable. I think people recognise that, but what happens once you have taken your vest off and put your kit away, is unknown. I view my day in terms of 'Was it a wonderful shit day or a bad shit day?' Dependent on which type of day it was, I go home carrying an emotional backpack with me. If my backpack is full, I've had a bad shit day and I will have flashbacks to the day's events, I will hear metal smashing, vehicles crashing. I'm trying to play with my kids, but I'm still buzzing from what's happened.

It's hard to eat food and settle down. Many bobbies turn to booze to forget and relax. If I have brought an empty backpack home, I can settle down and forget the day. That doesn't happen often. You can't stand with someone who has just lost a hand or a foot in a collision, walk away and say it hasn't affected you. It's hard to just forget it. I don't think anyone can stand face to face with death or see someone seriously injured in a car chase and continue as if it hadn't happened. If it has involved me, I will take home the negativity from that event. I take the victims of crime home regularly in my head.

In between we may do a school fete, meeting the kids, teaching them something. It's great, but it's rare. It's usually the negativity I see. The longer my time in the force, the more I realised that work and home were becoming merged. It's a hard strain. You wake up in a morning trying to be positive for what you have, your life and your family, but then everything you are dealing with is negative. Something must give somewhere. That something was my mind.

It's not all negative, I have also experienced laughable events, like the time I was coaching a partner. Two young Asian lads we had been pursuing, abandoned their car and made a run for it. I ran after and apprehended the driver whilst my partner went after the passenger. To escape, the runner jumped a wall, landing in a river. He began flapping around, screaming 'I can't swim'. Showing no regard for his own safety, in jumped the trainee officer to discover the water came no higher than his waist. He showed great bravery. It could have been different. He returned to the station sapping wet. I left it to him to explain his reason for it.

There is little I haven't seen, like the occasion when me and my oppo were in Oxenhope driving a country road. I noticed a black shadow by the passenger side window. I stopped to look again to see a kangaroo hopping alongside the car. It turned out to be a wallaby that had escaped from a nearby farm where they were being reared. I even winked and waving at it, as it hopped alongside the car before I thought, 'what the fuck am I doing…. what the fuck am I seeing?' Such incidents, alongside the times when someone comes up to shake your hand and thank you, make the job worthwhile. Sadly, they are far and few between.

HANDCUFFED EMOTIONS

I need to ask you to use your imagination at this point. We used to have allocated cars. Now my car was and still is my pride and joy. It is polished and vacuumed to within an inch of its life. It's part of me, it knows me, and I know it. I even named it Christine. She was a 58 plate Vauxhall Vectra. My baby. This was after the possessed car in the 70s movie of the same name. Well, she had gone into a police garage for a service during which they gave me a rubbish old Volvo T5 as a loan car. It was riddled with electrical problems, wasn't as fast or good as my gleaming Vauxhall Vectra 2.8 twin turbo rocket machine, Christine.

Christine was finally returned to me at 9.30am. To my disgust and horror, they hadn't cleaned my treasured possession. I spent three hours bringing my pride and joy back to pristine condition and ready for the road. Now, bear with me on this one. So, here I am, sat waiting, and a call comes in. I get a report of a man walking close by who appears to be confused and lost. Seconds later I am on the scene and talking to the person he tells me he is from Blackpool, that's a long way from home I'm thinking. When I check there is a report of a missing person. I get him into the car.

BENJAMIN PEARSON

A big smile spreads across his face. He is in safe hands. He complemented me for the cleanliness of my car. I beamed back, feeling smug. I didn't smile for long, about three miles from the station I smelled what I describe as mouldy cabbage mixed with badly cooked hamburgers. The odour intensified, I realised it was coming from the back seat. The male still had the wide grin on his face, but now a big wet patch had appeared in his crotch area. You've got it. Not only had he relieved himself in my beautiful car, he had also shit himself. It was leaking badly from the back of his pants. I raced back to the station where they placed him in the shower area and allowed him to scrub himself down. I returned to the wonderful Christine to find his thank you gift spread across her back seat. It was back to the Volvo whilst my car was clinically cleaned.

That was not the most embarrassing moment I ever had in a car. That occurred when I was in the Bracken Bank area of Keighley. I was chasing a small 'bag of crap' pool car worth about £200. Left, right, left the car went with the two 16-year-old lads in it. Just to add to the fun, they drove through a grassy area, getting ready to decamp. I followed too hastily, my Volvo sank through the mud and grass to come to a stop in a large soil pile, now lodged beneath my engine.

HANDCUFFED EMOTIONS

I knew I wouldn't be able to pull myself off so sheepishly. Feeling an idiot at getting my car stuck, I called in 'Hotel Tango 23'. 'Go ahead Hotel Tango 23' came back the voice from the control room. 'Yeah HT23, I'm stuck in a field and I'm trying to pull myself off, but I can't.' I whispered in a hushed voice. Now anyone seeing the car would have known exactly the mess I was in. Not the comms office. 'Pardon me HT23, you're in a field, trying to pull yourself off, did you say?' All I could hear was laughing, loud raucous laughter. Then a female cop shouted up.' Show me as attending, I've got full protection gear and a rope in case in all goes wrong. I also have the sergeant's permission.' They are all in hysterics with laughter as reality dawns. OMG, what the fuck have I just said. They have broadcast it over the full West Yorkshire Operational Pursuit Channel that I'm asking for someone to pull me off…. as quick as they can. I couldn't face that girl again without blushing, and I had the piss taken out of me for months after that.

Games People Play

It doesn't matter the job you are doing, when you face trauma day after day, you confuse what's real and what's not. Your own reality becomes merged with the reality of the job. Every call to attend a crime scene starts the adrenaline surging. You do not know what you will face. Will there be fatalities to deal with? Will you or your partner face an attack? Most of the public are aware of the deaths and injuries that make headlines. Most know about Roger Brereton shot in the Hungerford Massacre in 87, Sharon Beshenivsky murdered in Bradford, attending a robbery and Ian Broadhurst, a Leeds Traffic Officer shot when approaching a stolen car. For every one that makes the papers, there are many more that don't.

There is also the recognition that for some public, the police are there to abuse in whatever way they deem fit. There was one time, as a beat bobby, when I ran into a burning building. Bystanders shouted that someone was still inside. I didn't hesitate; I entered the three-story house. There was what I would describe as a bonfire lit in the downstairs room. I ran up the stairs to the second floor but within minutes the fire had become an inferno and I was in danger of being trapped; I shouted up to the top floor, no answer. I had to decide, did I risk dying in the flames by continuing or get out. I kept shouting out, but still no answer. I felt I had no option but to get out, only to find the premises had been empty all along. I risked my life for a joke. False call outs are not uncommon, people play mind games that push us to the limits continually.

As a police officer, you do the opposite to what a civilian does in a dangerous situation. If I see a man armed with a knife, a fatal collision or people trapped in a burning building, I run towards it, whilst others are running away. The reaction goes against all human logic, but it's automatic. A switch goes on in your mind, you react. Protect the public, its built into all officers. My heart is racing, my adrenaline pumps me up, moving me forward. All I think about is what I need to do. I make my decision. There is no time for hesitation, no turning back. I am in another sphere; I am in automatic pilot mode. Eyes are on me; I need to perform in a professional and speedy manner.

Next, I'm on my way back to the station to make a report. The adrenaline has stopped flowing and my thoughts are taking shape. I question myself, asking did I act in the right way? Could I have acted sooner, saved someone who died at the scene? An incident can be over in minutes, but the after thoughts last for days. Playing with your mind, disturbing your sleep. Why do I do it? It's like a police officer has the mentality of a lemming. If one jumps off a cliff, the rest follow. We don't think about consequences. Once you are in mid-air, there is no turning back. You keep going even though you are aware you are risking everything you love and know and even your own life. If you cock up, it's down to you. You then face the wrath of the public and an investigation by the professional standards department. It makes your decision that much harder, but it must be made, and you are the one making it.

There is a public expectation that says, 'Call the police, they will sort it out'. You are a protector, the 'go to' man in a time of crisis. You are also the fall guy if it all goes wrong. When I am out on the streets, I know that I am looked at with respect from some but with disdain from others. Has this changed over the years I have been in the force? Most definitely.

There is a stronger lack of respect amongst youngsters, often fuelled by alcohol and drugs. You'll find a lad who is a respectful kid when sober but becomes the world's toughest MMA street fighter when under the influence and showing off in front of his mates. Group mentality plays a part and puts cops in danger constantly.

BENJAMIN PEARSON

A call out to people dressed in black with balaclavas on, or a pub fight that turns into a small riot, puts you on a knife edge. You have little idea how it will turn out. Who will make the first move to be the 'big man'? Have they been drinking? Are they high on drugs? What mood are they in? Is anything stashed in the car? It's like facing a living time-bomb, one wrong move and it goes off big time. You can forget CCTV, kids today are savvy, they know where to gather out of sight. To some kids it's huge respect to get arrested, it gives them street cred. This is not only from their friends but also family members. Even granny has served her time behind bars. A good car chase, or to clock an officer. They become heroes. The more they do to us, the more respect they get once in prison.

When there is a lot of hate towards you. It makes you feel less safe. I know that there are people out there who would want to hurt me. It changes how I live my life; I go into certain pubs and avoid others. I've even been working out in the gym when I've heard. 'Pig.' Looking around, there is a man whom I stopped many times for driving like a 'dick'. He's giving me the evils. I have also had times where someone has recognised

48

me as a police officer. He then gets a few drinks down and comes in for a challenge. In an instant, I'm back on duty, my free time stolen from me. A younger copper might handle it differently, but with age I realise that the best way is to reason with them or walk away. I have the disadvantage that I am easily recognised because of the natural white streak in my hair. A condition I was born with.

People see you differently when you are in the force and whilst a lot disrespects you, there are also a lot who respect you. Your position, your role, your uniform, all prove to be attractive to some people. There is an aura of respect that also grows within you. Age is a bonus. The older you get, the more mature you get and learn how to communicate more effectively than when you are younger. Calming a situation down rather than winding it up. Some of the best days I have spent were when I was Ilkley, having an ice cream with members of the public and their children. I was showing them how the traffic car works. Seeing the joy in their eyes and smiles on their faces as they push the blue lights and siren buttons is magic.

As a policeman, the saying you must be all things to all people when dealing with the public is an understatement. You are a powerful authority figure. The need for compassion, empathy, calmness is all important. To deal with crowd control, issuing warrants, prevent criminal activity is a given. Dealing with the emotions of someone you have just held hands with whilst they have died is awful, and now you know you must inform their relatives. It's a part of the job I find very hard.

When you knock at a door, knowing you are about to change someone's life forever. There is no telling how they will react to you. Who the person is you are breaking the news to; you have no idea, but you are aware they will remember the day you came for ever? They will remember your face as the face who broke their heart. They will remember your smell; it will remind them of death and hurt. They remember the way you sat; your professionalism etched in their hearts and minds. They will ask the common question: 'Did they suffer?' It is hard to answer that when you have seen the car they were in, wrapped around a tree. There is no joy in bringing pain to someone's door. When you walk away, you leave some of yourself behind with the victims. Trying to ease their pain just amplifies your own.

HANDCUFFED EMOTIONS

The mental strain is great. You can go from total control on a job to an emotional wreck within minutes. The latter being seen only by your loved ones or in your downtime. Constant adrenaline rushes through your body in ways the public don't see. Energy from your blood and internal organs is re-directed to prepare for flight or fight and leaves your immune system weakened. This can cause ulcers and even DNA damage and premature ageing, not counting the psychotic episodes associated with PTSD. Little did I know then, I would soon experience this first-hand. Yet, this is all in a day's work for me.

So many changes have taken place since I first joined the force. Technology has moved on, but we still have outdated laws which haven't moved on. We must manipulate them to fit. The internet has made it so easy for criminals to look up 'how to commit the perfect murder' or 'how to build a bomb'. They are also up on the law and how the criminal system works. They use everything to their advantage. It all serves to make my job harder. They quote the law on you and think it's all a joke. They goad you all the time. 'Can't touch me pig, I'll sue you.'

BENJAMIN PEARSON

There is so much red tape. Hurdles, you must jump. Changes in the ways you can make arrests. You can stop the vehicle, but you can't search someone without grounds to do so. You may know that the driver of the car is a known criminal with dozens of lock up's and intelligence against him. He may deal drugs that are probably in the car, but that knowledge is inadmissible unless you have grounds to stop the vehicle. In all cases, we must observe protocol. Wording on reports based on the intelligence that give grounds for the search.

There is an independent panel now that 'dip sample' stop searches officers have done at random. They check your case record and any complaints against you. It's a catch-22 situation. You are damned if you do and damned if you don't. It all changed with PACE 1984 (Police and Criminal Evidence Act). All crimes are now occurrences, and everyone and everything that has been involved must have an occurrence number. When I first joined the force, I felt we were ahead of the criminals. Now, I feel overtaken by the criminals. They are so switched on and have access to a wealth of knowledge about police procedure and the law. I must be accountable, they do not.

HANDCUFFED EMOTIONS

One thing that really boils my piss is when I have arrested someone, and I take them into custody. They are continuing to abuse me and every other copper around. Their behaviour is appalling, then they scream for their solicitor. They also receive a copy of the Police Powers and Procedures from the custody sergeant. They get their phone call and due respect. All the time they are laughing at us. They are unemployed; never worked a day in their lives. We pay for their solicitor through the legal aid system. You and me and the person they have just burgled.

They know you can't question them once they have asked for a solicitor. We must then disclose to the solicitor the evidence relating to the offence and arrest. What happens often, is that three mates will be in the cells and use the same solicitor. That solicitor will brief them separately, but suddenly they all have their stories aligned. The disclosure has been discussed with each of them and their stories set straight. They have put together a readymade defence, well-coordinated between them all. It will then get kicked out of court. Hundreds of police hours wasted. They tie our hands; we can do nothing.

When you are working with an outdated criminal justice system, you are also working with outdated sentencing laws. I don't think a lot of the punishments given out fit modern-day crimes. The Criminal Justice Act of 2003 outlines four types of sentence statute specified in England and Wales. Discharges, fines, community service and custodial sentences. The criminals are more than aware of what crime fetches what sentence. A lot views jail as an easy option. A place where they can learn new criminal activities and meet up with their pals.

If it were my choice, prison would be where the offender was locked in a cell 23 hours a day. There would be one hour of exercise and no mixing with other inmates. I would turn lights out at 9pm and wake up would be 6am. If the sentence was five years, that is what you would get. None of the 'good behaviour' bollocks. They would behave out of respect rather than to get the sentence shortened. The Government moans that the prisons are full, so we alter the way sentencing takes place to free up space. Well, the criminal element will not go away. We won't get to the stage as in the film 'Demolition Man' where there is no crime. We need new improved prisons built instead of the billions spent on special projects. Then the reprobates would fear rather than laugh at the law.

Facing Loss

As a Traffic Cop, I came face to face with many fatalities and horrific sights. I knew that they were affecting my sleep and causing me to have nightmares. I just dismissed it, I considered that every police officer must be the same. That I was becoming ill never entered my mind. I had felt the emotional side of my job for a long time, but just accepted that it was part of the role. A part you had to get to grips with. No one ever talked about the emotional effects that being in the force has on you, and neither did I.

HANDCUFFED EMOTIONS

When I first became a traffic cop, they stationed me in Keighley, then Toller Lane; we were a special unit and treated with respect from fellow officers. Then we moved to Bradford around 2012, and I felt things changed. The camaraderie amongst teams in Ops didn't feel the same, but I was still with an exceptional team of lads. The best there is. I don't think they treated us with the respect we deserved at Bradford. When you are based at Carr Gate in Wakefield, the world is your oyster. The jobs and toys are there. At Bradford, they forget about you. You feel like the ugly relative who doesn't get invited to nights out in case you embarrass the family. They bounced us from pillar to post; it was like being back on beat but in a fast car covering the whole of West Yorkshire. There didn't seem to be any teamwork. They ran us into the ground, wanting more with fewer officers.

I realised then that I was feeling needy, and that wasn't the person I was. I had never been insecure, but that's the way I felt. I didn't want Milly, my partner, to leave me and I experienced tiredness and found it hard to get out of bed. I was lethargic and questioned if I had cancer. This leads to some strange thoughts. 'What's wrong with me?' 'This isn't normal, is it?' 'It can't be?'

As time went on, I noticed that what I saw as standard office banter was hurting me. Normally, I would have laughed off any comments. Now they seemed like personal attacks, but I couldn't understand why. I know coppers have banter, it's a way to relieve stress and its harmless. To me, it was changing. I was taking everything personally, becoming hypersensitive.

Without realising, I had segregated myself from the team. I would eat my meals away from everyone or not come back to the office at all. I made excuses to be away, so people didn't see me. My sense of humour, a trait they knew me for, disappeared. I was in the early stages of depression, but I didn't know it. It went on for months. I had no recognition that they may relate it to the brain injury I had suffered prior when being rammed in 2011.

As I've mentioned earlier, I see police time in three spans. The first up to 11am, the second up to midnight. Finally, the early hours when the real evil element are active. The blowtorch burglars and night prowlers. Now I'm a big man at 6'2", strong and fit and had always been the first to go in at the sign of trouble. It didn't bother me; I had a job to catch criminals, and it didn't matter what time, night or day that was, but I found that I was lagging by 6pm and I didn't want to go on nights. My energy wasn't there, and I worried the way I felt would hinder my effectiveness. I just felt scared thinking I would not come home.

Whilst those were the early signs, I didn't realise the reality of what was happening to me until after the death of my mother in 2017. When you live with trauma every day of your working life, you become hardened to its impact. You tell yourself that this is the job you chose; this is life, but it's outside of the inner sanctum where your family life lives. If that makes sense. So, although I had seen horrific deaths, none were personal deaths. My mother was different.

My mother and father had suffered a life changing trauma. They had been subjected to an assault in an armed robbery during which resulted in my mum's leg being badly broken, her thigh bone. She spent weeks in hospital and never got over it. It affected her walking. The incident had traumatised her more than anyone realised. She went from a smart woman, completely in touch with whom she was to become subdued.

Her fashion sense changed, and she stopped looking after herself. She had lost her vitality, drank more than before the assault and was happy to receive two bottles of wine as a present before a bottle of good perfume.

Mum's death was a shock to all of us. It was New Year's Day in the early hours of the morning; they had rushed her to hospital with what they described as a burst stomach. I now understand that she more than likely had a perforated bowel. Either way, it wasn't good. They had operated on her on and she was in the HDU ward. From there they moved mum to ICU, and they ventilated her. I knew from my police experience with hospitals that this was serious. I also knew that dad didn't really understand what was going on.

To cut through the niceties given to waiting relatives, I approached the staff and asked them to treat me like a police officer and tell me what was going on. They explained that her condition was profoundly serious. They were doing all they could. She had been in hospital 11 days when she appeared to have a re-surge and began talking. The evening before she died, the strangest conversation developed. She told me to call my little boy after my great grandfather and his middle name after my grandad. It surprised me. My partner wasn't pregnant. It was after mum passed on that she became pregnant. We had a boy and carried mum's wishes. It's something I'll never forget.

Seeing her talking and beginning to respond to those around her gave us fresh hope. It was short lived. Her organs were shutting down. The day after my talk with mum, I got a call at the station. I had to go to the hospital. A colleague 'blue lighted' me there. My brother had more of an idea what was happening, but it confused our father. I found myself in a situation of both police officer and son. I recall asking the doctor to be upfront with me and tell me what he would do if this was his mum. His eyes told me the answer. I spoke to my dad and brother and they agreed with me; it was kinder to turn off her life support and let her go. We gathered around her bed, holding her hands. I knelt and told her it was okay for her to go if she wanted to. It broke my heart to say that.

I faced a painful reality. This time I wasn't the police officer telling a stranger their son or daughter had been killed in a traffic accident. This was my mother, and I was telling my father and brother we should end her life. It filled me with guilt and anguish. It was overbearing. My partner arrived after they had turned the ventilator off. We left the hospital, and I held my partner's hand, full of remorse. I felt the heavy burden of the one who must decide. It was a load I knew I couldn't take anymore. I wanted to be a sheep rather than the sheep dog. I didn't want to be the one doing the telling, I wanted to be told. I think it was then that my older brother saw I wasn't holding it together. He took charge.

I think he saw something I didn't see. He did a massive thing and really stepped up to the plate. My dad didn't know what was going on. Dad wasn't stupid. I just think the shock of it all, and it moving at a thousand miles an hour confused him. I felt a weight lifted from me when my brother took over the arrangements, and I find it hard to remember anything that happened between my mother dying and the funeral itself. It's just a whir. Everything went so fast. It seems bizarre thinking back I was the one who would normally be in complete charge of proceedings and move everything forward. Now, I couldn't recall any of the events leading up to my mother's cremation.

I know that three days after my mum died; I returned to work. I wanted to go back. The sergeant asked me what I was doing there. I told him I wanted to work. He told me to pick my stuff up and go home. It's a weird thing after facing a family death, something in you wants to get back to normality. Normality for me was work. The Inspector came into the office then and ordered me to go home and not come back for at least two weeks. I left the building and remember nothing until I was pulling up into a car parking spot at my mum's funeral.

I remember reversing into the space and my dad saying. 'Let's do this'. I looked into his eyes and saw he was heartbroken. It hurt me so much that he was in a lot of pain and he didn't want to show it. I couldn't help him. It hurt me more than feeling I had left my brother to do everything. I saw myself as a bit of a failure because I couldn't contribute as much as I wanted to. I was sat on the outskirts of it. My brother showed me how strong one man can be in the face of bereavement. I was, and still am, immensely proud of him.

I knew I was still carrying around a lot of rubbish from a fatal we had attended two years before. It had involved a Porsche. It had been a warm May evening, and I had just started a late shift. They called us to a terrible collision on Otley Road,

Eldwick. I knew that the road was notorious for serious accidents. It was an area we attended regularly.

I rushed to the scene and I could see a vehicle with light rear end damage. There were people stood at the side of the road, talking to each other. I pulled up and began speaking to witnesses. I was told that the other car involved had gone. It had left the road. I thought initially they were telling me the driver had made off from the scene. Then I noticed tyre tracks leading across the grass, disappearing over a six-foot gap that led to a heavily wooded area. The silver Porsche was on its side in the woodland, smoke coming out of its rear. I shouted, ran across the verge, and jumped into the void. My colleague joined me. He was shouting to me to ask what I needed, meaning Fire, Ambulance, etc. These units are automatically dispatched once the officer at the scene radios to say, 'Fire to expedite'. In police speak it means 'The shit has hit the fan'.

I ran around the top of the vehicle, now underneath the car and facing the road area. The driver was still inside. A calm still look on his face but unresponsive. There was no way I could get him to safety myself, so I checked his pulse and administered CPR. I could feel the car rocking. It was unsupported, rested on its side. Stopped from falling by a heavy 9" branch that was also impaling the driver to the seat. His injuries from it were fatal.

In time, the emergency services arrived and extracted the driver from the wreckage. He was lying on the floor and being checked for ID so we could inform his loved ones he wasn't coming home. The chill that sends through you is bad, but I am used to seeing horrendous sights, so that didn't bother me so much. What really got to me is that his mobile phone vibrated and rang. On the front screen, it said WIFE. My heart sank. There was a family waiting for daddy, or hubby to come back. I know he won't and that their lives were about to change forever. They don't have a clue. I got an awful feeling, as if I were being sucked into the ground. I had this knowledge, and I felt I didn't have a right to know, nor did I want it. It was becoming a burden my mind was struggling to apprehend.

The Family Liaison Officer informed the family and came to the office to see me. The experience was strange he told me. When he got to the house, the wife told him she knew. They were packed waiting to go on holiday when one child said that daddy wasn't coming home; he was dead. Freaked out, she had rung his mobile phone. The call I saw at the scene. I started shaking, my hands sweating. It was like I was watching myself from another part of the office. I could visibly see the timeline and how many lives were affected. Every time I drive past that scene, my mind will remember the word WIFE on the phone.

That was the baggage I was carrying around with me and then the death of mum. It was too much to handle. It wasn't surprising when I think about it now that it was during this time that my nightmares and awful dreams got worse. They became heightened, more vivid. At 62, mum was young, and I was full of guilt. The decision to switch off the life support tore me up. Dad was in genuine pain and I couldn't stop it. Things were becoming merged. My role as a copper and a son were becoming one.

Two weeks later I was in the doctor's office pouring my heart out. They diagnosed me with depression. I knew I was struggling. All the thoughts raging around my mind. I was becoming ill but still didn't realise what was happening to me. I had taken pops at people. It wasn't me as a person. I was changing, and I knew it. I can see myself now in the doctor's office saying that I'm really struggling and crying openly. The doctor told me I needed medication. Now, these are what my dad has always called 'nut job' pills. I was from a stoic Yorkshire family, an alpha male. I didn't need pills to make me happy. I had always been happy as a kid.

When I started taking these tablets, they completely and utterly messed with my head. Once they took hold, I found that all I could do was sleep. After that I felt completely numb. I wasn't sleeping at all then. By the fourth week, I was feeling more like the old Ben. Finally, it was like a switch went in me. I had no fear, literally. I was living in a dream. I would go to work and where before I was doing 120 mph, I was now pushing 140 mph and where I wouldn't wrestle a big bloke; I was now jumping on him. My terror of heights disappeared, and I would go to high places and feel no fear. I thought, 'They are pushing something aside here, trying to numb something.'

Shortly after that, an incident happened that I will never forget, and will always have nightmares about. I had returned to duty and been told to take it easy, find somewhere to sit and think. It was early February and my compassionate leave was over. I had parked up in my patrol car. It was an icy winter's day when a call came through for someone to assist. The incident was half a mile away, and I felt the sweat on my hands; my heart was racing. I was willing another unit to answer the call, but none did. The call came through again 'Assistance needed'. The controller reported a traffic accident had occurred. In a panic, I knew I had to respond. It was a child. It could have been my child. I had a duty to the public. I was bubbling inside and I didn't know what was going on. I can only describe the feeling I was experiencing was as if I was sitting on a roundabout. It was spinning as fast as it could, and I couldn't stop it. That was my reality.

There was no one there to tell me what was going on. I had a void, a big void, and I couldn't see a way to fill it, yet here I was in my car, doing my job. No leeway from anyone. They were throwing me back into a traumatic event. My radio is beeping me, 'collar 1965. Where are you?' I want to scream. 'Fuck off, my mum has just died'. Can you leave me alone?' It makes no difference. There was no one there to help me check if I was okay. I felt alone, but I had my job to do.

They showed no compassion to me, they all knew I had just come back from bereavement, but it was just get on with it.

HANDCUFFED EMOTIONS

Normally I would go into automatic robot pilot. It's bred into you in the job but this time it was different, I put the car in gear; I took it out. I remember thinking 'fucking hell this is not right.' My driving was like shit. I couldn't focus or function normally. Simple tasks were just too hard. I was arguing with myself, clicking the car in and out of gear. 'I'll go, I can't, no, I'll go. I fucking can't.' My mind was everywhere. I thought in my head about the worst-case scenario. My knowledge platform. Everything I knew about my job disappeared. I remember it came across Romeo 1,2, Romeo 1,2, don't go. It's a child fatal. I was already at the scene though by then and they were letting me though. I couldn't answer my radio. I drove through a row of cars, then I saw a big 18-wheeler, 44-ton truck where the road crested to the right.

Members of the public waved me through the scene. Then I shouted over the radio....'child fatal.' A few metres from the truck lay this little dot in the middle of the road. It looked like someone had dropped a jacket on the floor. I shouted code 6, which means I have arrived at the scene. I got out, I could hear screaming and saw a bewildered truck driver in deep shock. Then I realised it was a little boy about two years old. I could see the detail on his clothes. His little hands were face upwards in that natural little curl that toddler's fingers make. He had a patch of brown hair. My daughter has the same brown hair. I shouted for more units; this is a procedure in a fatal accident.

As I got closer, I could see there was just a tyre mark. He had no head, no face. The top part of his skull had exploded with the pressure and was smeared on a nearby wall. The wheel had run through his head. I couldn't help him, there was nothing I could do. I felt useless; I daren't touch him because in my mind I would hurt him if I did. I could only cover him with my jacket. I asked someone to find his parents as he was alone in the road. I could hear sirens. Two women firearms officers turned up. I asked them not to go down. One did, and after a few minutes she came back up in tears.

It was too much, I just started crying. I could feel my legs on the floor, but I couldn't feel any other part of my body. I looked up and there were about six people just staring at me. Lights and sirens going. I thought they were saying 'don't panic, the cops are here! We're okay now! But why is he crying?' I remember they were shouting at me on the radio, but I couldn't move my arms. The ambulance and air ambulance arrived. I heard the control room shouting, Ben needs help here. Someone put an arm around me and walked me to a car to sit down. The only thing I could think about was my daughter. It was like I was seeing her lying there. It filled me with grief; I couldn't save my mum and now I couldn't save my child. It was like a black mist was towering down over me.

When I think back now, I recognise it was when I was standing about 10 feet from that little boy and could only feel my feet. My arms felt like there was an iron bar beneath my armpits and it was being squeezed, stopping the blood flow, giving me pins and needles all down my arms. That's when it went. It felt like an elastic band had snapped and ripped me in two. I couldn't feel anything because there was nothing left to feel, it had gone. I experienced real dread. Nothing would be the same, my life wouldn't be the same. Something had died inside of me. I knew it would not come back. I sat in the car and a temporary supervisor came over to me and said 'Right, just go back and do the paperwork'.

He could see that it had upset me, and that I wasn't right. I was hurting, but I just got put in a police car. It's bizarre because we set off back to the station and were going about 15, 20 miles an hour, but it felt like we were going 120. It felt like everything was rushing past me, but nothing was going past. I couldn't comprehend what I'd just seen. I couldn't comprehend that people needed me and in a time of need I wasn't man enough to stand up to the plate. I couldn't be there for the little boy. I kept thinking what if I'd had got there quicker, what if I'd have done CPR, but I knew it had already killed him? I feel like I've let him down. I know I haven't, but I feel that way.

No one sees the horrors we must face, and no one can know how much it affects us psychologically. These are things we live with, day in and day out. Then I ask, why should they, I didn't know either?

Do I Really Sound Like That?

Police Interceptors is a documentary that profiles the work of the elite traffic cops. It is also the programme I am recognised in public for. I had already had encounters with TV stardom. Making appearances as a police officer and border agent in the soap, Emmerdale, on at least ten occasions. That was back in 2010. I also appeared in the crime drama, DCI Banks as a cop. It meant that I already understood the technicalities and pressures in programme making.

Police Interceptors was different, though. It involved me doing my 'real' job in 'real' time. Initially, I backed away from appearing because I felt that enough people knew I was a bobby. My white hair streak was already identification enough. Then a few cameramen came into the office and wanted to film with our team. Two of my colleagues had already filmed, they seemed to have a natural flair for television. One had a cheeky side and the other was a confidant Jack the Lad; they were perfect to be in front of a camera.

I was content just doing my job, but one cameraman wanted to film my oppo and me. I was hesitant, so I agreed to drive the car but said I wouldn't speak on camera but when you are in a high speed pursuit or at the scene of a traffic accident you don't have time to think about camera's, you get on with it. On route the cameraman was nice and natural and made it simple. We had a laugh when my oppo mucked up and I realised it wasn't so bad, so I said I would think about it. After a conversation with my partner, also a copper, I said I'd do it.

Then the genuine fun began. I couldn't swear or show any bias on camera, so I had to be aware of how I talked and be careful of the banter we usually have. I have to say it took me a while to reign in where your copper's suspicious mind takes you and stick solely to the facts. I was told I had a cheeky flair about me. Funny looking at me now. The camera guy felt that I would have a big following because of the way I dealt with things. Ironically, I never wanted to be well known or famous. If you look at all these celebrities now, I just couldn't cope, but acknowledgement for something nice is a wonderful thing.

Being approached by children and asked for an autograph or picture, I find bewildering. I don't take it for granted, but if I can install a positive image of the police in kids, the kind installed in me when I was young, then that's good. To be a positive role model they can look up to rather than seeing us as arseholes in uniform, so showing no respect. It's important to show them that there are nice bobbies. There is a feeling today that all coppers are bastards and they're not. It's more important to me I give out a positive image than being famous. That's what I want to be known for. That's what I took away from the programme, plus how stupid I sound with my broad Yorkshire accent.

We started in season 15 and it went stratospheric. It was one of the highest viewed programmes on Channel 5, reaching

BENJAMIN PEARSON

1.7 million viewers. I couldn't go anywhere without being recognised. It was just mental. The fan base was so wide, from doctors to lawyers to architects, celebrities were even fans. Suddenly they recognised you from TV. The day-to-day criminals also watch it. The shit bags like it too.

I remember an incident the same day I was in Ilkley, buying an ice cream. It was a lovely summery day. I was with the cameraman and he said, 'that's Jonny Brownlee. He's an Olympic champion. Look, I'll show you a photo of him.' I noticed the guy was looking at me as I was looking at him, so I said. 'Okay, go on, I know you, don't I?'. He said, 'I know you'. It was so comical it continued like 'You're him, aren't you?' with him repeating the same to me. Being honest, I told him sorry, but I don't have a clue, he said 'I don't have a clue either'. We both laughed. It's so surreal. We both recognised each other from TV but didn't know where from. I found it bizarre that people look up to this person on TV, yet I'm the one he recognises.

You get recognised in the airport, on holiday, in the streets. Everywhere you go. As soon as they see the white streak in my hair, that's it. They come up to me. I have no problem with that, and I have experienced good things I wouldn't have done without the programme. Appearances on radio, meet and greets, car shows. The thing I don't like is, I also get recognised when I am with my family, my two children, although the eldest knows I'm on TV, it's still daunting to them. People don't know how to approach you and instead of being normal they thrust themselves at you. Try to hug you tight. Kiss the kids on their heads. I don't want my children involved in that way. They are young and how scary is it for a child when a stranger tries to kiss them as they've known them forever?

I'm not knocking being on TV and admit there are some enjoyable things. There are a lot of laughs but being on a 'reality' show is not like acting. There is a job to do and that job must be what you are focussing on. You don't have time to think, 'Do I look good for the camera. Will I come across well to the viewers?' I forget the camera and crew once I receive that call to attend a traffic accident or some other incident. In an instance, I'm immediately in full copper mode, ready to react, adrenaline rushing. There are no second takes; you can't get it wrong. There are lives at stake, and that can include yours and the camera crew riding with you. Knowing what you are doing is being televised can add an extra dimension of pressure in an already pressurised situation.

The idiots loved being on camera. You would pull over Billy Jo Shitbag and he would realise the cameras were on and it would be 'Ho, yes. Look at me, I'm on telly. You wouldn't catch me if I were in my Lamborghini.' Well, you're not in your Lamborghini, are you? 'You're in your Ford Fiesta.' The bluster was unimaginable. If you turned to them and said okay, you have 15 minutes of glory on you go. All they could utter would be 'Yer......... I'm a Bradford Star, Westside.' They didn't know what else to do. Nothing extraordinary ever falls out of their mouths. Intelligence bypassed them a long time ago.

Not all criminals react like that. There are those who go quiet and are aware that millions of viewers are going to be watching them and listening to all they say. They won't be able to deny it at a later stage. Acting like a dickhead with your mates filming it for You tube is one thing but acting like a dickhead for millions to see, doesn't quite bring the glory they are seeking. The show also gets us a new respect from some hard balls out there. They see we aren't as bad as they think, and we are nice. They will cough up to what they've done. It's hard to deny it when it's on camera. They just want it to be over fast.

Everyone wants to see what's going on when there is a camera about. Cars stop, people gawp at you. Seeing Channel 5 on the cameraman's vest top is not something they see every day, but they all know it's a TV crew. Most know of Channel 5. It's a normal reaction. It takes me back to one time when me and my oppo were driving through Thornton in Bradford and we saw this big tracker thing'. The one on wheels that carries the big cameras. There were boom arms on it, cameramen filming. It was all going on. Then, this big tracker thing with no number plates swings a hard left. We are on it immediately. I put the lights on as I follow it. It's then I notice a lot of passer-by's giving us dirty looks, as if to say. 'What are you doing?' I'm puzzled and look to the right and there stands Gabrielle Burns, the Hollywood actor. His mouth is wide open, staring at me. Still oblivious, I smile at him and comment to my oppo. 'Look there's Gabrielle Burns'. We realise then that we've driven straight through a film set. They had all the permits; the roads are all shut off apart from this

Trolley Dolly. We shout 'Sorry, Sorry'. Thankfully, they wave and laugh at us.

The reality is we all look up to stars, admire them and wish we were part of it so when people come up to shake my hand I don't mind. Problem is, they don't know what to say to you then. Their normal personality changes and they mumble out of embarrassment. It's funny really, and I wouldn't have believed it until Interceptors. Being recognised is great, but I wouldn't want it every day of my life and everywhere I went. I love it though when my daughter's friends shout out 'Interceptors' when I'm at the school gates.

It's not all fun, though. There was a time when I was on duty, when a man came up and asked if I knew Gareth Gates. I said yes. 'He's down there in the curry house and he's getting started on.' We went down and he's there with his girlfriend, surrounded by ten lads all abusing him. Basically, he's come in, they've recognised him and then they've seen he's got a Mini car. Now, in those days, a Mini was a big thing. He'd got a Cooper S, so they call him, 'Flash bastard, who are you showing off with your money?' The lad had done nothing, but he was a celebrity. That was enough for them.

HANDCUFFED EMOTIONS

Police Interceptors is different, there is a respect for the officers who appear on it. They know we are bonafide cops. We won't stand hassle from them. Give us shit, you'll get it back tenfold. We know also that people watch Police Interceptors for several reasons. Some because they see the real side of traffic cops or see that not all police are the same as what they perceive them to be. Others because they like your personality. They see we are approachable and that there is a funny side to you. Others because it brings danger into their lives. They see a side of nature they don't and hopefully, will never know.

There has been a lot of good positive publicity from Police Interceptors, now in its 17th series. We are no longer the nasty guys. It has changed some public perceptions but having a quiet beer in a pub with friends can be difficult. For that reason, I hang around with other bobbies. Even in the gym you get your name shouted out and recognition and the number of friend requests on media platforms I get, runs into the hundreds.

The film crew gets a lot of unfamiliar experiences out of the programme. Anyone who has watched Interceptors knows that they hide nothing. The incidents are real, and we react to them as we would without cameras. We stage nothing. The car crashes and violence shown when apprehending criminals are happening in actual time. Drunk drivers, car thieves, high-speed pursuits all take place whilst the cameras are there. The film crew experience them with us.

The film crew also see the dangers we face when trying to do our job. In episode 1 of series 16, I attend a crash scene with my oppo to find a car has flipped over and landed on its roof. My job is to help trapped passengers or see if there are any fatalities and to secure evidence at the scene. The number of lookers-on who are too busy filming on their mobiles to recognise they are further endangering lives can hamper this. It's more than frustrating when you try to move them to a torrent of abuse.

Another episode involved me in a top speed pursuit in Bradford. I was in the driving seat when a car went speeding past. I put the blue lights on in the rare hope that he would pull over. No such luck. The driver put his foot down, and a pursuit began. I requested TPAC authority but had to abort when the car drove the wrong way down Manchester Road. Lives would have been at risk if the pursuit had continued.

We picked the car back up later. The driver was being reckless; He was driving through red traffic lights, across the front of other cars until his wheel punctured. Still continuing, he crashed into parked cars. Refusing to give up, he legged it. Me and my oppo were immediately out and on his tail. I found him hiding in a bush. After tackling him to the ground, I took him into custody.

Waiting for a van to pick up him we faced a group of laughing and jeering locals. The criminal got the kudos he wanted. He risked the lives of other drivers. Searched, we caught him in the possession of class A drugs. It landed him 16 months in prison and a five-year ban. To those who do not know of the risk's criminals will take to get away, this may seem extreme. It isn't, it's an everyday event.

The lack of respect shown to the police doesn't stop at criminals. An incident happened in a garage. I was trying to apprehend the driver of a car that reeked of cannabis. I opened the door to get the driver out when a woman in another car screamed at me; I was blocking her exit. She became abusive. That I was doing my job to protect the likes of her, meant absolutely nothing. There would have been a time when the public would have thanked the police for acting to apprehend a criminal. That has now changed.

There is also a genuine need for us to be careful what we say when they are filming. It's not just the criminals. We must curtail the normal banter. One time I remember was when me and my oppo had a conversation, well it was more of an argument. It was about Santa Claus. I was saying. 'What do you mean he doesn't exist, get a grip of yourself?' Wound up, he was arguing he didn't exist, so I said that he was telling all the kids in the world that Santa didn't exist. We carried on about how his sleigh was magical and he had special dust he sprinkled. I was winding my oppo up increasingly and he was biting. He began going into the technical details such as. 'Why doesn't Santa's house show up on radar?' 'Because you have to believe, that's why, stop being stupid.' My oppo was at a screaming point by this time, and then we spotted a drunk on the side of the street. 'Pull over', he screamed. He pulled his window down and said.' Excuse me, sir, who comes on the 24th December?' The immediate answer was 'Santa Claus.' It was hilarious. And then the realisation dawned on him he shouldn't have said all that on camera. Ruining poor kids' dreams.

It was during the time of filming that the cameraman assigned to us, who became a friend, started noticing that I was up and down. We'd be going to jobs, and I'd be shouting at people in a bit of road rage. He talked to me off camera and said they would cut some things out and explained that I was being very direct with suspects. Not rude, but more aggressive than normal. The problem was, I couldn't pretend anymore. I was getting so tired and it takes so much energy to pretend and lie to yourself. So much energy to pretend you are normal. I was getting lethargic. The invisible bags that I was carrying around with me were getting heavier and harder to carry.

I used to ask myself, 'I am an officer with no fear, pretending to be a normal member of society, or am I normal, pretending to be an officer with no fear?' Either way, I was lying. I had lied to myself and others about how I was feeling. I didn't fully understand it. I knew I depleted my energy, even my oppo recognised the changes in me. The cracks were showing. I started having black spots with seconds missing. It wasn't until later I realised that I was showing signs of PTSD.

Accountability is key in the force, and the radio commentary we make is a key part of that. Senior officers review it along with other officers, once back at the station. They picked up that I was missing things and making slight mistakes, which wasn't like me at all. I was swearing at other drivers rather than concentrating on my driving. My attention span not focussed in the way it should have been.

One review they did took place after what I saw as a good, fast pursuit. I thought I had done my job well, but slip ups were seen, so driver training got involved. They gave me words of advice. None of them could understand what was happening because they knew me so well and this was totally out of character for me. I was told that unless I changed, I would have to go back for an advanced driving refresher course. I was feeling lost but didn't see where I was heading.

Tasting Real Grief

Amidst all the traumas and horrific events, I have encountered throughout my time in the force, none have affected me in the way the death of my father did. I was already ill by then and still in grieving for my mother.

He was special to me, incredibly special. He worked in the building trade as a ceramic tiling technician. The hours were long, and he always said to me he never saw me until I was 14 years old because of the hours he spent in work. I remember he was always out working, never at home, but at weekends he made up for it. He loved his snooker, and we used to go with him to the Con Club and watch him play. He'd buy crisps and pop and we'd sit with mum whilst he played. They were some of the best times.

As I got older, in my early 20s, he became more of a friend. Mum was always the matriarch, the one who chastised us, parented us whilst dad was at work. Dad was fun loving. He used to come out drinking with me and my pals. Thinking back, it was funny; the phone used to ring to see if dad was coming out with me and my brother. No one saw him as my dad, but one of the boys. My mates loved him being there as much as I did. He was just accepted as part of the group.

Even when he lived in Spain, he used to come back over here to do tiling jobs; he was so well thought of and in demand. Then he would come out with us lads again. My brother and I had moved out to Spain with him and mum, when I was 9 years old to be near family. My aunt Viv had married a Spanish man and was already living in Spain, and dad wanted to get a bar out there. Majorca was like a second home to me. It was also the place where I experienced bullying on a big scale, once again, because of my white streak. I was English in a Spanish school and different. It was the early eighties, and they didn't know what to say to me, so they called me 'Horse'. After a while it got a bit too much, we would turn up at school and get beaten, day after day. Now, it's probably different. But then there wasn't an international school with multi languages. We were the only English kids in the school alongside 1000 Spanish students. We were the obvious targets. The only language spoken there, by pupils and teachers alike, was Spanish. I learned to speak fluent Spanish, I had to. I can understand it even now, well a little of it.

We stayed there a year before moving back to England, but then mum and dad went back to live there again in 2000. That's when he moved back and forth to do jobs, see us, and come out with the lads. I saw him then, perhaps once every 6 months. By the time I got to my late twenties, early thirties, it had become the norm. Just accepted as that, we were best friends. I remember a time when he came over and landed around the 10th December. Mum was still in Spain and dad had work to do here, right up until Christmas.

BENJAMIN PEARSON

I remember there were just us two in the house and he hadn't had time to get me anything as a present. We were about to go out and celebrate Christmas Eve when he disappeared off to ASDA. He had bought me a Spiderman DVD. Didn't wrap it or anything before we went out. That night we got smashed. He could hardly stand up by the time we got in, but he rushed upstairs, got some wrapping paper, and wrapped it round and round the gift, including his arm. He then got Sellotape and did the same again. By the time he had wrestled it from his limb, it looked like an enormous ball of mesh. I could see the disc half hanging out. He threw it under the tree. Next morning, we got up and exchanged gifts. The sight of mine was so funny we just laughed until we cried.

It was a crappy present, but that didn't matter. The thought behind it, and his need to wrap me a present for Christmas, did. It then became a challenge every year who could buy the World's crappiest presents. Silly things, plastic knives and forks or a pack of batteries. I once forced both him and mum to wear baby bibs and silly hats for the whole of Christmas Day. One drunken night had brought about what became a family

HANDCUFFED EMOTIONS

Christmas tradition. It was great. These memories are the wonderful ones I have. It may seem silly to others, but to me, they are the special things that make families special.

Others include the 'lads' holidays we went on, dad always with us, one of the lads. There was one time we went to a villa to celebrate his 60th birthday. We have always had this massive friend's thing between us. It was bizarre, which I didn't recognise until he wasn't there, but he used to ring me every day to touch base. We were genuine friends. He would have to visit the house every day he was here, only for ten minutes, but he needed to do that.

It was 2010 when my parents came back from Spain and they both felt they were missing seeing their family grow up. I was with Milly by that time. Dad had always wanted a daughter but never had one, so when our daughter was born, he was smitten with her. He did everything he could to be the grandad to her he would have been had she been his daughter. He was besotted. You could see in his eyes he saw her as the daughter he never had. He never left her side, he was there when she walked, took her to the park, did everything with her.

BENJAMIN PEARSON

When our son came along later, Milly noticed that my dad was going to the doctors a lot. She began questioning it with me. He had two lumps on his nose that turned out to be cancerous. He didn't see what was coming. Nor did I. He had them scraped off, but to him it was then fine. That was the way he was. I wondered if it was because mum had died just six months before.

I put it down to the fact that dad had been thinking about his own mortality. He wanted to make sure he was fit for his grandchildren, and that's why he was going for check-ups. At that point he was having checks for everything. Dad believed nothing would happen to him. He had a thing about needing to make sure everything was all right. He wanted to be a young grandad, which he was. All he wanted was to see his grandchildren grow up. Be there for them.

One day he came in, sat on the couch next to me and said, 'I have something to say to you'. I thought nothing of it. Dad was always a joker, but this time it was different. Looking at me, he said, 'I've seen blood in my pee.' He'd had an operation to scrap lumps away from his stomach and they had found cancer. My first thought was 'is it something I have to worry about?' It was stomach cancer. He assured me that a bit of chemo and it would be fine. We aren't a family to cry and see the worse. So, I accepted it and thought he would be all right. They cure many cancers today, don't they?

A few weeks later he returned and asked me to sit down. I knew something wasn't good. They had confirmed the cancer to him, and it was terminal. I was numb for a long period. He said that the chemotherapy would enable him to live longer, maybe two- and a-bit years. He was 67, then I thought, 'well, two-and-a-half years. You can die any time; I had learned that through the police.' In my mind, I could die from a heart attack tomorrow. We had a further two and half years with dad.

I became concerned; he had lived alone since mum had died and sometimes, I thought he must be lonely. With my bobbies' hat on, I was fearful that some scum bag could break in and hurt him. He would ring me up and come down to the house for hours at a time, so he wasn't lonely, but he was still 67 years old. I was pushing 41, but still strong. I knew I could look after him, so I tried to get him to come to live with us. It didn't work; he enjoyed his own freedom. Milly knew that better than me. He needed his own space. We had to let him live his own life rather than become stagnant in ours. On reflection, it was the right decision. It wouldn't have been the best thing for him. It took a month for everything to sink in about what was happening. He had his chemo, but minor things were happening all the time. He seemed to have one little thing after another. One procedure followed by another procedure.

He began his chemotherapy once they had his blood levels right, but it made him so tired afterwards. It would boost him back up but then he would be low again so they would give him another blood transfusion. So, to me, I noticed nothing different. He always seemed fine. It was when he began coming more to our house; I noticed how ill he was. He would have something to eat and then go into the toilet and vomit. His weight started coming off and he got tired often.

I realised I had false hope, and it was a false reality. It would not be all right. My mind was telling me I couldn't lose my dad, that couldn't happen. Dad then asked us to go with him to see the doctor. I was so angry. It was a doctor specialising in cancer, but he did not understand how to speak to people at all. I remember him saying, 'There is no simple way to tell you this, but the treatment hasn't worked. There is nothing we can do.' I've seen the same on films and TV, but people are told in the most compassionate way. Not my dad, he was told bluntly, as if his car had just failed its MOT and was ready for the scrap yard.

I've seen so much death and destruction as a cop, I didn't get upset. I saw it was just another hurdle to get over. I felt sorrier for my dad; he had an idiot dealing with him. One shaking as he spoke. It didn't fill me with confidence. This was my father, a man I loved, and we were talking about his life with a doctor who was shit. We walked out, and I grabbed one of dad's hands, my brother took the other. I remember saying that we would all be there for one another. Dad said, 'Onwards and upwards, there's a lot more out there worse off than me.' We said no more, we got in the car and drove back.

It hit me that night. 'hang on a minute, this is done.' I was working up to 80 hours a week, different split shifts. Fatalities, accidents, and the rest of the crap out there. Milly was doing the same, so I didn't really comprehend how much we value time and how it goes so much faster or slower than you want it to do. Now it was passing quickly. Dad's physical form was changing so fast. His weight and strength were going. From a man who always loved his food and ate hearty meals, steak, red wine, he changed to a man that wasn't enjoying his food anymore. Now he had reached the stage where he needed support and we knew it. The best option was for him to move to my brother's house where there were the facilities he needed.

In the September it was dad's 68th birthday and although he was ill, he organised a party and invited people I hadn't seen in a long, long time. He had been told not to drink, but at his party he started drinking, chatting with his friends. Trying his best, determined to enjoy himself. I knew how much it was taking out of him, but my brother and I also knew his reasoning behind it. Dad was saying goodbye in the only way he knew how. Standing back watching him, I realised how content and happy he looked that night. I don't know if his guests knew how ill he was. If they did, they weren't saying. It was just how dad wanted it to be. A final 'get together' to remember.

Dad got very ill a few months after the party and became mostly bed ridden. Mentally, he hadn't given up, but it was hitting him that his body was now giving up. It hit me hard. I was hurting. One day, a close family friend who I saw as a second dad, came to visit him. Dave was a fellow police officer and a hardened man. As he left the bedroom, I saw it upset him. I knew this wasn't Dave. Then he burst into tears and hugged me. 'I can't come again Ben, I'm heartbroken. I can't see him like this.' At the same time as this was happening, dad's best mate Richard was also ill and died shortly after him of cancer. I like to say they couldn't bear to leave each other.

We got dad's affairs in order. Banks, his will and we'd be speaking to him and he would start to mumble. I knew then his mental state was going. Dad had one wish, and that was to arrange his own funeral, and I would make sure we carried his wish out. It didn't matter how long it would take to get the information from him. It would happen.

Ironically, before that I had been at a fatal collision in Wilsden. This man came out, asked me if I wanted a cup of tea. We chatted, he told me he had retired, but was a funeral director. Making light of the situation as bobbies often do to cope. I told him there was some work for him now. He laughed, handed me his card, and told me if I ever needed him. I thought it weird, why would I need him. Little did I know it would only be six months later that I would go to him for help.

The respect and the way he had treated me at a harrowing scene told me I could trust him.

I recall his daughter coming around and being bemused. It was the first time she had dealt with someone before they had died. I introduced her to dad, and he told her exactly what he wanted. His songs 'Never Walk Alone' and 'Spirit in The Sky' by Doctor and Medics. He expressed to her he wanted to write his own eulogy. I wrote it with him, and we got it all down. It was so funny, in true dad fashion, he ripped apart everyone in there. Once finished, he felt he had everything done he needed to meet his wishes.

I think he knew then that his time was near. He came to us for Christmas. On Boxing Day, he collapsed in my front room. He had waited to see Christmas with his family and his grandchildren. I took him back to my brother's then, and we knew we had lost him. Bit by bit he was fading. We lost everything from him. By January, I had to take time from work because of the stress. The force doesn't help here at all. You can only take a few days dependants leave to look after your dying parent, then it must be your holiday leave. My brother stepped up to the plate again. We have always been close, even though we are different in our ways. I listened to dance music, him, Guns and Roses. We were like chalk and cheese. I went to work, saved my money. He went to work, blew all his money and got into a lot of fights. We were so different in our outlooks.

I was proud of my brother; he did everything for my dad from washing and feeding to dressing. All he could to make him comfortable. I was working long shifts, feeling the pain of my dad's suffering. Once I'd finished, I spent hours by his bedside, playing music, talking to him until he got to the point he couldn't talk. Blinking was all he could do in response. He would say odd sentences, but he was out of it most of the time. A week before he died, he stopped eating and going to the bathroom. The McMillan Nurse came and explained it wouldn't be long but just make him comfortable. His body had failed, and he had retracted into himself at this point. It hurt him if you touched him. His body had ceased up. The only function he had left was his ability to blink.

You understand that I was watching all of this as a son, but also a hardened bobby. I didn't want to cry or shake. I'd lost my mum, but I'd got no port of emotion. That's the price you pay as a copper. The day before he died, a best friend from the force sent me a text to say his dad had just died. Now he was one of those mates who, hearing that, you would ring straight away and vice versa. As heart breaking as it was, I had to reply telling him I was sorry, but I couldn't deal with it. I couldn't support him with his dad's death when mine was at death's door. I got 'okay' back. I know that must have destroyed him, and I will always be sorry for that. I am sorry to this day. I should have been there for you, John, for that I am deeply sorry. I got to sit with my dad for months. He didn't.

Dad died at about 1pm in the afternoon. There was just my brother and me in the room. Just before he passed, he mumbled, trying to have a conversation. It was like 'I love you; do you remember when we went to the seaside?' A brief chuckle came out. It was a last conversation, a peak before he died. Mum had done the same. His breathing got shallow and slowly he passed. We never left his side. I knelt by his bed and promised that my brother and I would always look after each other. As he stopped breathing a wave of pain came over me. I couldn't breathe, I hugged him. At that moment everything came out, and I cried. I have never cried as hard as that in my life. It was like I had a red-hot dagger piercing through my heart.

When you spend time with someone you love. Someone you know is dying but you can care for them and make their last days comfortable, it's all the sadder when you know there are many others who don't get that opportunity. I see it every day. Mothers, fathers who never got to say goodbye to their sons or daughters. Only a copper faces that grief continuously.

You must remember I wasn't thinking straight, I was already becoming ill, and it was affecting the way I looked at things. I think when someone is dying of cancer and suffering and you are watching them lose who they are more each day, you almost feel relief when they die. I was like that with dad, but I felt immensely guilty and ashamed for thinking that. The rational side of me was being taken over by the emotional. I just didn't want him to hurt anymore. I don't know if there is a Heaven or a Hell, I really don't but I think there must be something. I just wanted my dad to be with my mum. That's all I wanted for them both. I hope there is a beam of sunshine filled with a pure love that they go too. Idealistically, I would love to believe that there is a door you go through and all your loved ones are waiting for you there. I think most of us want to think like that.

I remember the undertaker from Wilsden came. Now I've been there hundreds of times and I know how they deal with dead bodies. I asked him to remember to treat him with respect; he was my dad. He nodded, gave me a big hug. I know from experience and I hope people reading this book will understand when I say it's not nice the way some of them treat a dead body. It's like a piece of meat without a soul to them. I must also state that the conditions of some bodies they must deal with make it hard for them to put it into a body bag with dignity. Then they must manoeuvre the bag through the door, which can be very narrow.

No one enjoys having to deal with an accident fatality, suicide, or murder victim. Imagine trying to get a dead body, already stiff down the stairs, around furniture and through the door. It's not dignified. It's like a cluster fuck. Doors banged into; banisters bumped. It was important to me that didn't happen to my father. I knew they would treat him with respect, and they did.

The next day we had the terrible job of clearing out all his stuff from my brother's house. Why so soon you might think? My brother Leyton and his family had seen enough. It was important that the house became normal for them again and painful as it was to do it, that's what we did. Some reading this may not understand that, but none of us could really face looking at his stuff every day. I didn't want a shrine to dad. My brother didn't want rooms of stuff reminding him of the pain dad had gone through. It's not what he would have wanted. Dad was a firm believer that when you have gone, you have gone.

As it ended, he admitted that it scared him because he didn't know if there was anything. It's a question we all think about but cannot really know an answer to. The hardest part for me of dad dying was re-tracing the life he had. The walks in the Park, the nights in the pub. There was a void. A void left in the lives of so many. I saw the respect he had in the community at his funeral.

BENJAMIN PEARSON

The day of dad's funeral came, I looked around at some members of the family that I hardly knew. Laughing and joking and telling me 'we were family'. It annoyed me; I didn't know these people. Dad's relationship with his parents had always been dysfunctional, not talking to each other and all that crap. So, now I'm faced with strangers telling me how much we needed each other as a family, was an affront to me. Family to me is someone that I can call at 3am and say I need help and in an instance, they are in their car on their way to me. It had never been like that with some members of my father's family, and we saw little of them.

When you stand back and look around you realise who genuine family and friends are. Loyal friends you can usually count on one hand. They are there for you come thick and thin. I think it's a fact in life. The internet has given people the impression they have hundreds of friends and it so easy to forget what genuine friendship is. My touch with TV stardom showed me how easily others flock to you and want to be your friend, but it's a surreal thing. I'm fortunate enough to have people around me who really care and are there for me. Dad had friends like that.

HANDCUFFED EMOTIONS

Mum's funeral was nice with about 80 people attending. Dad's was different. In the crematorium it was standing room only. Many mourners had to stand outside of the closed doors listening to the service, they just couldn't get them in. The place where we had the wake held around 100, but it was jam-packed, you couldn't move in there. There were people whom I had never seen. He had been a rocker in the 50s and 60s, and they had all turned up. Building trade members, family. He would have laughed to see that, but also, he would have been proud. It was also standing room only in the crematorium, with people having to line up outside.

The service itself was unusual. You remember dad had written his own eulogy. It went something like: 'How are you doing everyone, Steve here. Sorry I can't be there but I'm busy but if you want to knock on the box, I'm in. I'm not getting up though.' People were laughing, hearty laughs he would have loved. He continued to say. 'I've never hit my children, I left that to their mum, she beat them black and blue but not me.' There were quips in there, aimed with precision at friends.

They applauded it at the end and he well deserved it. In line with his wishes, everyone had turned up wearing an item of bright clothing to show how much they respected him.

People use the term 'when he died, a part of me died'. I think some say that lightly. The same with 'trust me.' It can be so fake. When I say part of me died, I mean part of me died. I knew I was next in the firing line. There is a certain pattern in life we expect to follow. It's mum and dad, you, your kids and so on. Mum and dad had now gone, and I was now on the top layer. Its natural progression. You realise you're an orphan and top of the food chain. You are not young anymore. Your mortality is in question. Usually you are 60 plus when this happens.

Here I was, a 41-year-old and the next branch. It's not something you can take lightly. Both parents have died in their 60s. The state of my mind was telling me I had 20 years left. I would not see my kids grow up, walk my daughter down the aisle. There was a void there. I understood this happened to a lot, but I hadn't seen myself there. I was in a realm of surrealism. Everything I did, I thought about. Silly things like eating more cheese could give me a heart attack. Having a bit of steak because its red meat. Driving at 34 in a 30 zone because that bit more speed kills. This was exactly what my job required me to do.

At that point, I knew I had lost a bit of my soul. I wasn't taking it lightly at all. Turning up every day facing danger, you can't imagine that feeling when part of your heart has gone. I'll use an example. Imagine you are walking down the street near ASDA, you see an old lady fall over, what do you do? You go help. Then, see a 24-year-old shoplifter fighting with another man. What do you do? Most would answer, ring the police. Well, I am the police and it's in-bred in me to go forward, not back. So, when everyone else has run away I am going in, but who's there for me?

Both my parents have gone so who says to me 'I will be there for you; I'll be there to pick you up?' I'm having to go on duty every day and face that danger, but who will put their arms around my kids if I don't come back? Now if I'm in pursuit on the M62 of a stolen vehicle going 130 mph and I'm going at 130 mph; we must put a box on that car. There are three boxing vehicles coming up my rear. If a wheel on my car blows out now, I'm dead. My colleague is dead. There's no coming back from that.

I'm at the top of my game. I work with some of the best traffic cops in Bradford. The best traffic cops that you will ever see. Team 2, which I am on, and I'm not blowing steam up their arse, but they are the best of the best. You cannot get a better-trained TPAC pursuit specialist. They are the elite of the elite. I have been there when there are wing mirrors coming off. Paint and sparks are flying whilst you are hitting the vehicle to the side at 100 plus mph. We are hitting the Armco barrier and the vehicle is literally self-destructing in front of you. I am thinking, 'this is not what I'm meant to be doing in a car.' There's that bloke then in the other car that's got the balaclava on. He's looking straight at you. Has he got a gun, got a knife, or has he just killed someone? Why does he want to get away? Then there's your colleague in the third car who's looking at you, his face is saying 'don't leave me, just hold your ground.' You do what you need to do to back this up. The radio comms channel telling you, 'Box on. Box on.'

I am making split decisions; I know I have a role to play. Then the car door opens, and I am out on foot, I am after this lad. I must make those split decisions in my life and now I am running into danger, but I've got nothing in my heart to give. I have saved more lives than I can remember. Pulled people out of burning buildings, given CPR to dying victims. All part of my job as a good copper, but now I felt that I had nothing left to give to anybody.

Fall in front of me, I'll pick you up. If you're crying, I'll put my arm around you. You're hurt, I'll tend to your wounds. I'm bred to do this, but now I'm struggling to come forward. I'm scared that I'll leave people behind. I still didn't recognise I was ill. I knew I had negative thoughts, but I didn't put it all together at that point. I knew I was grieving for my parents and that was affecting my thoughts, but I continued my job as a thief-taker. A job I was proud to be doing.

A third pursuit comes, and your bandit car is doing 100 mph in the City centre. Your colleagues notice you are making mistakes, you are blowing junctions that you shouldn't have blown. Not driving beyond your limits but seeing things differently. Rather than being in the pursuit I sit at the side watching. I am telling myself I need to be slowing down. If the wheel veers or I hit a lamppost, I am finished. I felt that I didn't want to do this anymore. I'd give so much of my heart and soul, lost so much, and there wasn't one person there to put their arm around me.

It reached a pinnacle point; the consequences are real. It became as if I was on the edge of a cliff; I had one foot over, there was no going back. What do I do? Do I walk? Do I jump? Or say to my colleagues and friends, I can't do this anymore? This, I now know, was the start of my drive into darkness in my mind. I never realised that my body and my mind were telling me it was all over.

When I look back, I was being told by people that my comms was wrong. My driving was exemplary, but I was saying things I wouldn't normally say. My downward spiralling attitude was saying 'fuck it, I don't care. If I get home at night to my family, I'm not fucking bothered.' It's a hard thing to not only lose your family, but then to lose yourself. Unless someone has been there, they can't understand what it means to lose yourself. Everything you do, changes. The structure you have built in your life, in your partner's life. Picking your kids up, your Routine. What you do on a Monday morning or a Friday afternoon. The dinners you make for yourselves stop being meaningful. I had lost my identity as a person, and it wasn't getting easier.

The sack of stones, I've talked about before, is there. It's getting heavier. I can't comprehend or understand why. My direction in life is disappearing. I just feel hurt at the loss of my family and I think of all the lives I haven't saved. The young children whom I've seen die. The old people I couldn't save. It started coming back to me. I saw another Ben; it wasn't me; it wasn't the Ben that started as a young, naïve lad. I'm now that person who thinks I'm done here. I need to hug my children and my partner. I want to sleep; I really want to sleep because it's tiring.

BENJAMIN PEARSON

The Tipping Point

I have thought so many times, trying to recall the point at which I finally tipped over. I know there are several incidents I now have nightmares about, and I also know the two-year-old boy, killed by a truck, pushed me to the edge. The death of both my parents also affected me. Were any of those incidents the actual tipping point. I don't know. It's so easy to reason with yourself how it went wrong. I don't remember a time that I wasn't ill, it's been so long since I last felt right. I know it started with an insecurity. A vulnerability I hadn't experienced before.

I've already mentioned how I segregated myself from my colleagues, but it went further than that. They always saw me as the comedic one, I had nicknames for everyone. I was in an office full of alpha males, and I was the alpha male joker rather than the alpha male Hardman. A lot of the team called me Princess, they said I wore my heart on my sleeve. All was in fun, but I was now taking it personally. Team 2 were my colleagues and a great bunch, I loved working with them. I don't think they knew what was going on. They put my changing mood down to the fact I easily became emotional and nothing more. No one commented when my work ethic changed from sitting with the lads to sitting at my computer downstairs.

I always considered myself as a team player, I still do. I still felt loved for the character that I was, but I didn't feel like telling jokes anymore. I wanted to get in and get out of the office. I didn't have the energy to socialise and be funny. I was getting upset at silly comments I would have laughed at previously. I was in the early stages of depression but didn't know that. I felt a discomfort at the tiredness. I slouched, and my back and neck hurt. This was happening every day. I was looking forward to holidays and time off, yet I loved my job, it was my passion.

Working nights became traumatic to me. It's during the graveyard shift when you spot someone standing at the back of a house or in the garden with a torchlight on. They're watching you; they are wearing balaclavas. What crawls the streets at night would surprise and alarm any decent human being. I meet them all. I used to go into the dangerous areas of Bradford and come away thinking, 'I wish I hadn't seen that.' There is some creepy stuff that goes on, but I know it's what I'm paid for. My training provides me with the skills to deal with this. I was now finding it harder and harder to face the shit that's out there, night after night. I felt discomfort from the tiredness.

My dress and deportment standard that I had always prided myself on was slipping. I thought, 'I don't care what I look like. I can't be arsed.' This was happening before the deaths of my mum and dad. Something was already altering the way I thought and acted. My mind and body were telling me. 'You are finished.' I was already heading into a downward spiral. Then came the loss of my parents, which fused with the loss of myself. To lose yourself as a person, your identity and to not know yourself as Ben anymore is heart-breaking.

Dad's death had taken me to a new realm of despair. I had felt that I had handled the quick deaths of my parents, well. I was a hardened copper; I had seen death too much for the sight of dead bodies to affect me. I viewed it differently to other people. It was only when I went back to the doctors because I knew something wasn't right that I attributed it to mum and dad dying. I didn't think of all the traumas and incidents that had occurred before or the vital part they played in my illness.

In the doctor's office, I was in tears; I was shaking and struggling to breathe. I didn't understand what was happening to me. It was then that the doctor increased the dosage of my tablets. They made me numb. I felt that I had no more love to give people, even though I knew what love was. I've felt it many times. I had no feeling in me. I had no attachment to anything. I felt distant to what was going on around me. I could stand on a street corner and just the World go by. To me, within five or six seconds of it happening, it had passed. I just wouldn't feel anything. I couldn't remember anything. I was feeling lost. I can describe it for you by saying, imagine being small and standing in a glass box that is 6 inches thick. The box is in a black room. Zoom out about fifty feet, look how big it looks. Go to 100 feet, now zoom out again a good half a mile and see how it looks. That felt like me inside my head and heart. I was getting smaller and smaller, locked in a glass box surrounded by darkness.

In my head I was sitting on a little chair with controls driving my body. Everything was surreal. I had no inhibitions; I could say and do as I want. There was no punishment to what I was doing. I remember my son being born; I had always wanted to have a son. Pearson's' are all men, so I just wanted a mini me. The feeling of joy when he popped out, I cannot express. I was jubilant, but I felt nothing that was real. My body knew what to do but, in my heart, and my soul, I couldn't feel it. I was functioning physically, but not emotionally.

We had named our son after my great grandad and grandad. He also has the same name as the 2-year-old boy who died under the truck wheels. In my subconscious I merged the two. I wouldn't hold him or touch him. I didn't want to feed him. Not that I didn't love him or want him; I wanted him more than I can say. It just felt inside like I couldn't do anything. I was living in fear, every night I was going to bed dreaming of him dying or being hurt. I could see myself dropping him and him landing on his head or I would visualise waking up to find him dead in bed. My mind was so mixed up that I thought if I distanced myself from my son, I wouldn't harm him or feel the pain. I knew I had, by that time, stopped feeling pain, but something scared me about being with my son. My partner Milly noticed this, but I didn't.

It took me a good 7 months before I could feel comfortable with him. Before I felt that I was safe with him, I would not drop him, and I could take him outside with nothing happening to him. When I look back now, I remember the feeling of awe when I knew I had a son but mingled with that was the horrific thought of what I would do if I lost him. The state I was in, I would probably have done something stupid. In my heart of hearts, the distancing was a protection from myself. Now, I carry the regret that I didn't hold him more when he was a little baby, but I was ill. I was experiencing PTSD but was oblivious to it.

I feel that I have made up for it now, but you can't help being ill, especially when it's a mental illness. I had lost mum. Then the two-year-old boy incident occurred. My son was born then, but I'd never healed. Then dad told me he was poorly, and that's when the sleep issues started. All I was dreaming about was how my children could die. Things were going through my mind. If they were both swept out to sea which one would I save. If that happened, I would prefer to die myself, but I saw that was selfish, a coward's way. A 'cop out' from deciding. I didn't know whether other parents thought like this. You never talk about such things. I could hardly go into the supermarket, see someone in the frozen food section aisle and say, 'Hi, how are you going? Have you ever thought which one of your children you would save if both were drowning?' They would think you were a right fuck up, a nut job.

I would go to bed at 10pm. Milly would be asleep in seconds and I would look up at the ceiling. I would be like that for hours, even though I had to be up by 5.30am. It went on day after day, week after week. I decided to send a 'WhatsApp' to work saying, 'I'm struggling here. I'm not sleeping, I feel there is something wrong.' The lack of sleep was crippling me. When dad died, the sleep didn't really get much worse, but everything just merged. The pain and the nightmares intensified. It was nothing to do with dad, I was just at the point where I was still working. Still attending fatals, I was taking in more than my cup could take. It was overflowing and I couldn't stop it. I am trying to live a normal life. I'm filled with pain and anxiety. I'm failing to cope. I've got depression and PTSD. I'm going under fast.

I had this old sergeant, Rick. A true hero, he was smack on form, knew exactly what was going on. One sunny morning, I get my car keys, it's 20 degrees outside at 6am. I go down, check my car. I'm really car proud; it's got to be clean. The cleaner my car, the faster it goes. It doesn't, but it's about image. I sit inside, put my seatbelt on and my shades. The radio goes beep; I hear X-ray Romeo 1.2 and it's as if someone has dropped a 20lb weight on my chest. I suck into my seat. X-ray Romeo 1.2 and I can't breathe. I'm holding onto the steering wheel, twisting the rubber. X-ray Romeo 1, 2 and as I look up all the cars in the car park go smaller. I get tunnel vision, and I'm struggling to breathe. I remember I shouted on the radio, '1,2, bear with me'.

I know when I got out of the car; my left leg was shaking. My hands were shaking. I thought I would piss myself. I couldn't see properly. I nearly started crying, I was in full panic mode. I made it back upstairs to see my sergeant. I said, 'There's something wrong with me here. I don't know what it is, my head's gone.' 'Get yourself to the doctors.' He told me. He knew how much I was struggling but put it down to my mum. That man was one of the best. He could see I was having a problem. It was in a transition period; Rick was due to retire soon after. Mum had died, Dad had cancer. The little boy incident. They had made no diagnosis yet, but it was all coming to a point. I had also now lost the best sergeant I had ever had.

When dad died, it all becomes grey, I had time off, and naively thought everything would be okay. I put everything down to the build-up of all that had been going on in my life. One day my old sergeant rang me to see how I was and if I was ready to go back to work. He asked me how I was thinking about the job. I answered honestly and told him I didn't know.

I didn't. What I knew was that every time I thought about going back or talked to someone about work, I felt a fear inside. It was a real dread and a tightness, knotted in my stomach.

You are talking to someone 6'2", who has done martial arts, is strong and has no fear about going straight in when there is trouble. Running into a burning building, tackling the toughest hard guy. None of that scared me. The things I get scared about is someone saying, 'Ben, you have cancer.' I get frightened about things I can't control. Now, I was thinking differently. I had lost the plot. I told myself that I was ding, ding, cuckoo. I was mocking myself though because I never really thought I was mad or ill. I just knew something was going on with me.

When the bad dreams first started, I used to think it was like being in the advert I watched on television warning about drink driving. It depicts a man who wakes up at night and by the side of his bed is a little kid standing looking at him. It ends with saying, 'Can you see him now?' I can only think someone with PTSD wrote that for them.

That's what happens to me, I wake up at night. It's not a dream. Someone is standing at the side of my bed. For an instance I think 'someone has broken in. Is it one of my kids?' Am I seeing things? Am I having sunstroke of something? My mind is playing tricks on me. I see a grown man stood at the bottom of my bed, I jump out and try to grab him and there's no one there. These are people I can see and smell. They are tangible people; I can hear them breathing. I can sense death. In my sleep, I'd have a leathery taste. I'd be breathing in what smelt like old books, I could taste blood on the roof of my mouth.

I'd look down and see bodies laid on my floor. They would ask me why I didn't save them. Why didn't you have the same love for me you have for your own family and got there sooner? You could have saved me then. I knew I couldn't, but this was so vivid I questioned whether I could have got there sooner. Could I have saved them? Everything got twisted and merged and I couldn't control it.

I was also re-living incidents that had happened earlier in my illness. One stands out as if it occurred yesterday. It involved an RTC (Road Traffic Collision) with two brothers. It was one of the most horrific crashes I have had to witness. A beat car was in pursuit of them. They were driving dangerously in a built-up area; Then came a massive bang. They shouted on the radio, in a panic. 'CRASH, CRASH, CRASH.' We were close by, so we attended. The boys had lost control and wrapped their vehicle around a tree. So great was the force that the engine had left the body of the car to stop 150 yards past the vehicle. At its thinnest width, it crushed the car to 5" wide. This continued with the doors, seats, centre console, and the brothers. The injuries they received were horrendous. One was totally de-gloved, The other fused into him. I can only give the example of the Michelin man from the TV advertisement. I don't say that lightly, there is nothing remotely light about two pointless and gruesome deaths.

The car itself was unrecognisable. The impact of it hitting the tree had demolished it. It looked like it had been in a scrapyard and crushed into a small square. I had to escort the bodies to the hospital. They were taken into the resuscitation area, as I attempted to collect evidence. Their skin had rolled off their bodies, they were just muscle and bone. I had tried to identify them at the scene through fingerprints, but there was nothing solid on their arms to hold on to. How can you inform parents that they have lost two of their children? For what? It's a question I ask myself a lot. The incident went to an independent police commission, it had been so bad. The car had ripped a lamp post from the ground before hitting the tree. One lad died immediately, the other minutes later. The Coroner concluded that drink and drugs had been responsible for their deaths.

I find it hard now to look at a Lurcher without being taken back to an incident that occurred on Silsden Bypass. Two lads were in a Jeep that had broken down on an unlit road. It was hit from the rear by a transit van at 70 mph. Both lads had stood behind the jeep. The impact threw them forward. One ended up half stuck on the front of the van. The other was thrown down the road and was dismembered. A Lurcher was licking the brains of the deceased. Now, if you are gagging at that thought, imagine re-living it night after night and through daily events that occur and immediately throw you back to the scene. That is the existence I am living.

Such experiences prey on my mind, come alive in my dreams. I find myself awake in nightmares. The stench of death all around me. Eyes looking at me accusingly. The 21-year-old epileptic who crashed her car, the sill of which penetrated her chest through her neck. Visions of the little six-year-old, knocked over by a car and killed instantly. Laying there in her school pinafore and white frilly socks.

I'm not one to reach out to anyone. It's not in my nature I always work things out for myself. This time I sent a work WhatsApp. I suppose I was asking for help, but I couldn't say that. I'm struggling was as far as I could go. I could have reached out and said, 'Lads, I really need help here.' The problem is that whilst the team rallied round and gave me full support, a corporate officer pushed it up the line. 'Fucking hell look at this.' He must have thought. 'If he tops himself and I've not told anyone I will grab that brass rail.' So, where your friends may say. 'Come on, let's help. We'll go talk to someone.' Someone different would just report it.

Ultimately, someone had reported me. I felt as if I'd been shot, not in the back but in the front. I knew it had to be someone higher up. Friends would have been there for me, but things moved fast. No one came to me to say let's get you to see occupational health. Whoever did it was on a corporate scale because the thought was not 'come here, let's put an arm around you.' It was more like. 'Report him, get his permits taken off him, pigeonhole him and put him in a box. He's damaged goods, don't go near him.'

I come into work and I'm walking along the top corridor where the traffic office is. Most people are on the back end of the corridor, so I pass them. I'm coming along with this label stuck on my back. 'Brain dead, idiot, mental patient.' I'm getting looked at weirdly by other teams and officers who don't really know me. I walk into our office and instead of 'come here, sit with me, let's talk.' I'm getting these looks. I get asked by a supervisor from another team to turn out and I say, 'I can't drive'. I get looks. Then it starts. The questions, why can't you drive? I must justify why I can't drive. Someone else then asks me to go do something. I repeat that I can't drive. I'm ashamed of saying it.

Inside, I'm angry. If I couldn't drive because of religion or my sexuality or a physical illness, then they would accept it, and I would get all the support they could give. Because I have a mental illness, I'm stigmatised. All I get told is that they would put forms into occupational health and HR by a stupid internal system that failed from the start. I'm told it will be two days. Three weeks later I'm still in the office, a non-driver with revoked permits, still stewing over the fact that my head is all over. I'm seeing dead bodies at night; I'm not sleeping well. I've got chest pains; every day I think I will have a heart attack. My body is literally causing itself pain.

I feel isolation, I'm far from close to anyone. No one understands. All they think is that I'm weak. There is an attitude of, 'Why can't you cope? We can cope?' I don't feel supported by top brass or the organisation, but I understand with my team because no one knows what is going on. If I'd have been there and it was someone else, I wouldn't have known either. Today it may have been different, but no one knew I had PTSD. Everyone knew I had lost my mum and dad and put it down to grief. They just thought I was handling it badly. Didn't know what to say to me, how to handle me.

It wasn't grief. Day and night, it was killing me. Destroying me as a person. I can see how people could throw themselves off a bridge without a second thought. Luckily, I had Milly supporting me and three or four close team members who would tell me not to worry, they would drive the police vehicle and look after me. When I needed them, they were there, trying to hold my hand through it but not realising how bad I was. You also must remember that these people have their own jobs to do in the same way I had mine. If they come in one day and they don't talk to you, it's nothing to do with not liking you. If they don't ask you how you are doing, it's not an upsetting thing, it's because they have so much going on in their own minds.

I don't want to create a misunderstanding. My team and people on other teams supported me in so far as sending messages and emails. It's not the same though as the teammates who put an arm around you and show you, they are there by your side. Now one copper that showed me genuine compassion was a lad from a different cultural background to me. You hear all the time about institutional racism. But the only difference in him and me was our shoe size. We would hug each other, talk and discuss our lives; he was like a big brother to me. There were no barriers of any kind between us and that's how it should be amongst people, irrespective of colour, religion, or anything else.

HANDCUFFED EMOTIONS

The part I found hard was when we would go to a pursuit in Leeds and the local beat cars with the ANPR team would turn up. That's the automated number plate recognition vehicles. Now they are in plain cars and they class themselves more special than you are even though they haven't got the service or training in that my team has. We are traffic cops and get paid for what we know, but they would scoff and say. 'Why aren't you driving? We've heard you've had your permits pulled.' I'm stood there in front of four other work colleagues and a prisoner plus members of the public. Its soul destroying, but I wouldn't care. I'd just say.' Yes, I've got some mental health issues.' They would stand there with a look on their faces that said 'shit.' I would mock them and say. 'There's only four others and a prisoner with us, so don't worry. I'm fine about it.'

I would think this wouldn't be happening to me if it were something else. If I were transgender or I'm changing my religion to Buddhism, they would say nothing. I don't live in a namby, panby world. I'm not part of the snowflake generation, but you have no right to say that to me. If I must abide by the rules, be kind and respectful to you. You also must abide by

129

them. You can't say those sorts of things. Insult me and walk away without it hurting.

I wouldn't turn up at a crisis centre and say 'All right nut jobs, have you got some mental problems?' I wouldn't do that, you just don't. You have a level of common decency. Those officers had little idea of the danger of the pursuits I, or any other of the traffic cops, take to get the scum bags off the roads to protect the public. Nor did they know the nature of the trauma's suffered but felt they could take the piss out of me in front of others.

I remember one lad on our team who had a pursuit and the man he was chasing died. I've asked him several times how he is, and I can see the pain in his eyes 15 years on. Now, you can't picture yourself in that pursuit or know how he felt knowing the driver had died because of the pursuit. They did not understand the incident that haunts me to this day and always will. It was a pursuit that involved a dangerous lad in Bradford. Wanted for six armed robberies and carjacking. He was in a stolen car. No one could catch him. I'm on night duty, a single crewed officer. I'm driving around the rougher areas of the City. I was aware of an outstanding blue Subaru Impreza

HANDCUFFED EMOTIONS

STI, believed stolen by a violent offender. Every sighting had reported it had driven off at high speed in the Toller Lane area. I knew also that the driver was a trained boxer and was using his fighting knowledge in the robberies.

His fighting skills didn't worry me. I was trained in martial arts and could hold my own. I was also driving a Vectra 2.8i twin turbo, a missile on wheels. Undaunted, I began searching for him. At 3am, I'd passed a few vehicles, but nothing stood out. May as well go back to the nick for a brew. I'm at the red traffic lights at the junction of Hamm Strasse and White Abbey Road. It was a pleasant night, so I wound down the window and I could hear…. BOP, BOP, BOP, BOP. The unmistakable sound of a Subaru's 2.0 litre engine and open exhaust. I looked to my right. Two dull coloured head lights are approaching the junction at a slow speed.

Slowly it rolls out of the junction and I see the driver is an Asian male about 20–25 years old. He's driving with his sun visor down at 3.am, like any normal person would do. Not! He was sussing me out. As our eyes locked, it hit me. 'Fuck me, this is him. The robber and violent carjacker.' Adrenaline pumping, I grabbed the steering wheel. I know this will be a fast pursuit. BOOM………. He's throttling it down Hamm Strasse towards Keighley Road and Manningham Lane. The turbo on his car is whistling as he's ramming through the gears, light blue smoke is pumping out of his exhaust.

As I let out my clutch, the high-powered motor of the V6 kicked in. I did a U turn, turned on my lights and siren's. I was in pursuit. Over the car pursuit channel, I voiced. 'X-ray Romeo Urgent.' This informed headquarters that I was behind a Subaru that was trying to get away. The vehicle turned a sharp left onto Keighley Road. I locked on 30 metres from its rear bumper. I expected he would do a right, left, right, and then decamp. We both sped up, and I thought. 'This is going to be stupid; I need to think about aborting.' Glancing at my speedo it read 120 mph. I was in a 30-mph limit and was getting faster. Buildings were rushing by and the Subaru was gaining distance. I wanted it to end, but not with someone dead. He then crossed the carriageway onto the wrong side of the road and headed towards red traffic lights on Queens Road. His speed estimated at around 135 mph.

'Abort, Abort.' I shouted down my radio, pushing hard on my brakes. All I could think was. 'This is a fucking nutter. I'm not dying for him.' Seconds later, the chassis of the Subaru rolled to the rear offside. Everyone thinks they can drive when on a straight road but once you add in bends and corners, they're fucked. His car skipped across the carriageway, throwing up dirt, stones, and muck in the air. It then went backwards towards Oak Lane. The speed 80 to 90 mph. I knew he would not handle the vehicle, and I was 100% certain he would crash. I just didn't know that it would haunt me forever.

About 300 metres in front of me I saw an explosion of metal, glass, and dust. My first thought was. 'Shit, please let him be okay.' He may be a robbing shit bag, but no one deserves to be badly hurt or die. I was only doing my job. I got out of my car and walked towards what I can only describe as a small tin box on wheels ripped apart by a T-Rex on steroids. The Subaru had disintegrated on impact with a bus shelter and skidded 20 metres up the road before stopping.

A dark figure climbed out and ran into the darkness across the park. I gave chase. I zoned in on the driver. I heard no sound, no voices from the radio on my chest. All I could see was a shitbag running as fast as a cheater. My heart was pounding, and I was panting, and I knew there was no way I would catch him. I'm in combat gear with heavy pants and a stab vest on. My kit adds a further 20 to 30 lbs of weight. I gave up. I was now about half a mile from the crashed car. I could only wonder how he could get out of a car like that and run as fast.

Back at the crash scene, I saw officers flocking around a large mass on the floor. I approached; it horrified me at what I saw. The car had hit the wall at speed but there had been a young, fit 19-year-old lad sat on the top of it. He had been walking home from a night out with friends and was taking in the night air, having a rest. His bum on the wall, his legs dangling over. The Subaru had hit his legs and virtually ripped them off. There was nothing left of his legs. Severely injured, the lad was lying on the ground screaming for help. I stared at his injuries and just cried. This was my fault. I'd caused it. If I'd have gone for a brew and not pursued, it wouldn't have happened. Do you know the guilt and shame that places on your shoulders?

It's impossible to explain how devastated I was. They removed me from the scene and placed me under investigation so they could assess my driving. They rushed the young lad to the hospital where he had emergency, life-threatening surgery. Unknown to me, beat officers had found a blood trail and followed it back to the driver's home address. They found him sat on the steps of his house with a broken neck and bleeding heavily.

Following months of investigation, they cleared me of any wrongdoing. They found me to have done my job professionally and in accordance with my training. I was vindicated, but they had done nothing to take away the pain and intense guilt I felt for the 19-year-old. It was immense and overwhelmed me. I requested a meeting with the lad. I needed to beg his forgiveness. I remember knocking at his door. His mother opened it. Behind her, I saw him. He was struggling to get from the kitchen to the living room. A young man, his life in tatters. His legs shattered. He had undergone months and months of operations, rehabilitation, and therapy.

I stood filled with remorse yet, here he was, smiling. His eyes full of positivity. 'Chill, relax. It's not your fault, I don't blame you. The driver should have stopped. You were doing your job.' I cried and begged forgiveness. He shook my hand with the warmest of grips. He told me to let it go. I had done nothing wrong. I am still humbled by his attitude. His motivation for his future was unreal. His philosophy on life 'everything happens for a reason.' What he is doing now I don't know, but I hope his view on life is still the same.

They sentenced the violent offender to 8 years. It wasn't enough for the crimes he had committed. It turned out that when he had climbed out of the Subaru; the shitbag had climbed over the injured lad. He didn't stop to see if he could help or how he was. He could have been dead. All the driver cared about was escaping. He had crippled someone and didn't give a shit about the consequences. This is human nature at its worse.

Colleagues from other districts and departments would not know what I went through that night or the many incidents that had brought me to the place I was now in. They aren't there at night seeing the things I am seeing, yet here they were, airing my laundry for everyone to see. I felt betrayed and angry. I will never stop feeling guilty about that young lad, even with his forgiveness because I cannot forgive myself. I am there to protect the public, not to put them in harm's way.

HANDCUFFED EMOTIONS

If you're in a pursuit where someone dies or is seriously injured, you know that a little piece of you has gone. As a pursuer, you know what they are going through, so you are careful to support the officer involved. You would never walk up to them and say, 'Hey, have you killed anybody today then?' Yet, with mental illness, there isn't the same decency or compassion shown. It's as if you are a leper. You have something unseen that no one wants to catch from you. If there has been a fatal, you talk about it with respect, honour, with kid gloves. One of my colleagues this happened to will tell you he carries it around with him all the time. You sympathise, try to understand. With mental health issues, it's different. It's like a voodoo subject. No one wants to talk about it, and they leave you to stew. They categorise you as a headcase. I don't understand it.

Within two weeks of them pulling my permits, I knew I was going, in my head, I was going; it was just a matter of time. I was getting in my car and driving home, and I had nothing inside of me. It's the point when I felt, if a truck hit me now and killed me, I'm not bothered. I had nothing left, nothing to give.

No one is going to miss me. I'm just draining oxygen in the air that other people could breathe. It's wasted on me.

I know I'm not processing things as I should. I can talk to someone for 15 minutes, then I might leave and come back, and I start the conversation again. I have no memory of what I've said or who I've spoken to. I can see someone and say, 'Hi, I've not seen you for a long time.' For them to tell me I've spoken to them ten minutes before. My mind couldn't process what was going on. The lack of sleep, the nightmares, the diet where I'm throwing food down my neck just to have some energy and try to get on an even keel. The pressure and stereotype of what they expect you to be and the stigma you are walking around with lays heavy on your shoulders. It becomes unbearable.

I had got to the point by then that although I had a job I loved, I would do anything not to go into work. I just didn't want to face it. It was physically killing me, draining every bit of life out of my body. I thought I was going to have a heart attack. I could see them finding me lying dead on the top corridor at work. I knew it happened. Young, fit people, no health problems, just dropping dead. I thought that would be me. With the pains in my arms, it convinced me it would soon be over. I would be dead.

I knew I had to take drastic action to get something done. The system wasn't working for me. I felt I was in a system that didn't cater for mental health. I had tried to tell them I wasn't right, but it had now been three weeks, and I hadn't heard a thing. All I got was it must go through Occy health. Now, if I turned around as a member of the public and said I would slit my wrists and top myself, what would they do? It would be oh fucking hell. They'd panic, try to lock me up. Put a log on, he's doing x, y, z. And here I was weeks later, and no one had done a thing to help me.

How do you cry out that you need help in an organisation where you aren't a man if you show any sign of weakness? I had cried out; I had written twitter posts, WhatsApp's and talked to superior officers, being reported, and had my permits pulled for my trouble. I was angry that the genuine support I needed was missing. I was still going through the slow system of waiting for an occupational health appointment. It had been three weeks and still no notification of a date for assessment.

I then found the number for HR and rang them. I told them I'd been waiting three weeks to get an occupational health appointment. 'Sorry, can't help you. Everything must go through TOBY.' The police computer system that was already failing me. I was at the end of my tether. I said. 'Right then, if you don't get me an appointment, I will most likely hurt myself or do something stupid. You've got a duty of care to look after me.' I put the phone down and with minutes Occy Health ring and I've got an appointment. Amazing, I then thought if I had been someone weaker, I could have topped myself by now.

Then, I was out with my oppo one day and we got called to a bump in Rooley Lane. It was something and nothing. We turn up and there's a lad with a cut. I got out of the car and Boom! I didn't know what to do or where I was. I know I have my notepad and pen out, but what for? The switch has gone, my partner is measuring up and I'm thinking. 'What the fuck am I doing here?' I'm walking around and I knew nothing. It was like I'd never been to police training school. It was three weeks after they had pulled my permits. I'd officially had a breakdown.

HANDCUFFED EMOTIONS

We got back to the police station and people noticed that something was wrong. My sergeant came to me in the corridor and I was just crying, in hysterics. I was a shell of the man I once was. She said. 'You aren't right, are you?' I knew then that in my heart of hearts I'd had a breakdown. I'd had a mental episode, and I knew it had ended. This was the day it had all gone wrong. I left work immediately and went home. I could remember throwing all my gear in my locker. The gas, my belt and radio, all dropped into my locker. Something told me then that I would never use them again. It's all gone. Officer 1965 had ended. Even then, I did not understand how powerful it would be for me and how everything would start coming out and they would diagnose me with Complex PTSD.

A Cry for Help

HANDCUFFED EMOTIONS

Do I feel anger, you bet I do? I'm in a vulnerable state and no one is taking responsibly. I'm trying to cope with all these demons and all this hatred. A system is falling down behind me and they still left me on my own. I'm trapped with all the stereotyping, being pigeonholed and I'm being ignored. Why is there not a red button you can push? A 999 helpline. There is for everyone else. Why don't we have a system that works? I'm sinking, going under, and you don't care. You're compounding my illness.

If I attend a fatal, or potentially fatal, there is a system. I must submit forms and you put in a telex. That telex we send to the media unit, so a press release can be sent to the TV and Papers. It also goes to the Big Bosses, The Head of Road's Policing, The Collision Investigation Officer, The Sergeant's Unit, SOCO (Scene of Crime Office), so everyone knows what's happened. When I was in need, the one place it didn't go was Occy Health so they could say,' That's horrendous, the officer needs ringing to see if he's okay.' It does now, but too late for me. Now, they have put things in place to support officers.

They now have a system. They have brought in a TRiM practitioner; you can go to. Milly is one of them. It's stands for Trauma Risk Management. It's a method of prevention, used to identify individuals at risk of PTSD and other stress-related disorders after being subject to traumatic events. So, someone can say there's something not right with Fred, and Milly would then approach them and ask if she could speak with them. She isn't there to do anything but just to listen and assure them they are not on their own. If anyone else needs involving, she can then tell them where to go for help. Anyone who goes to a traumatic incident now gets a personal trauma manager to look after their wellbeing. Milly volunteered for this role because of me and what she sees me going through.

I was so upset by my treatment that I sent a scathing email to the Assistant Chief Constable. I never got a reply. But four to five days later a sergeant rang me to ask if I was all right. The sergeant she said she knew I had emailed out to the ACC, but it had been passed down the ranks to an inspector. Then to a sergeant and now I'm ringing you. So, why not just send a twitter message and tell me you're sorry about the system? Reassure me I'm okay, I'm being looked after? I felt betrayed by the service I'd given 19 years to.

HANDCUFFED EMOTIONS

If I were involved with a member of the public in a road traffic accident and I said to you,' ring on these details.' but I just ignored your call, you'd report me. If I didn't contact someone for three weeks, I'd get bollocked and I'd deserve it. So why can you leave me suffering and no one gets bollocked for not looking after me? I called out and asked for your help. If I'd have slit my wrists, if was a drug taker, seller, alcoholic or a thief, the system would come down on me like a sack of shit if I didn't do what I should do or behave in the correct way. You'd lock me up and throw away the key. So why can you brush me aside when I'm pleading for help?

There is no gap for mental health. It takes two seconds for that form to go digitally to Occy Health. It takes two seconds to ring a 999 number. The Force has numbers for dozens of different associations. The Gay Lesbian Association, The BAME Association, whatever association you want or need, but no number for mental health. Nowhere to say, 'Hey, I'm struggling, help me. It has gone too far.' You could say, 'well you can ring First Response'. No, I couldn't because I believe one of the first things they will do is put a log on me. Police could come around and may take my kids off me and try to put me away. That's why I won't do that. What I need is for you to put an arm around me. I need you to tell me you'll look after me and that I was one of your best. I got nothing. Nothing.

What really upsets me is that if I weren't who I am mentally, I know I would have done something to myself. I would have left my two children without a dad and Milly without a partner. Is it fair to put me in a role where you see all that I've seen and then not provide the aftercare that I need? Then, when I cry out for help, I'm abandoned. It feels like no one wants to come near me, and no one wants any association with me. I feel disgust at that. All they had to do was pick up a phone and say, 'We're listening.' I have more people speak to me now, stood in a queue because of Covid 19, than any that talked to me in the police about my mental health.

I'm not talking about my team when I speak of the lack of support. My team, Team 2 Traffic, know this, they have supported me endlessly. The establishment has betrayed my loyal service and hard work. I've lost so-called friends on Facebook, had others not talk to me because I have mental health issues. I am stigmatised because of what's happened to me through my role in the police force, and no one is holding their hand up and admitting they have done any wrong. I faced the things I faced because you have told me to go do those things. I've gone out and looked after people, taken on their pain, and shown them compassion because it's my job to do that and I have a big heart. All I wanted was for someone to show me the same respect and courtesy.

They have put me on TV. Made a programme that is one of the biggest on Channel 5, changing the way people look at the police and giving the force a lot of prestige because of it. I feel anger, genuine anger. To send a tweet, a simple 'We're sorry for what's happened to you.' Instead, I have my pay cut by half. Soon I will go to no pay. I have a mortgage, kids, a partner. Why? I'm not sat at home watching football; I didn't go out on my motorbike, fall off and damage my own legs or hurt myself doing a hobby. I have been damaged by doing my job. I should be told.' You've done well, and we will take care of you if you are pensioned off.'

It's like I'm a loaf of bread and I've got mouldy. Instead of cutting the edges off and trying to make something of it, I'm thrown in the bin and they buy a new loaf. I've fulfilled my role, there is no need for me now. I go back to that wavy line conversation from my trainee days. They have pulled me out of the line and a replacement will quickly take my place. They have failed in my case, but no one wants to admit that. Instead of looking after my wellbeing, it's easier for the organisation to brush it under the carpet.

I was told that the ambulance crew, who came to the scene of the little boy killed under the truck wheels, could go home. I had to go to the station, sit on my own and write a full report that took hours. That was the order, and I had to follow it. I'm sat at a computer screen alone thinking about this tiny child. The office is empty. No one came to ask if I was all right. I got no follow up to check how I was handling it, remembering that I had just buried my mother two weeks before. I had to continue next day as if nothing had happened.

It hurts, I've been there for so many people. I've been the person someone has seen before they have died. The last person they see. I made sure I was there for them when no one else could be. Is it too much to ask that the organisation I have given everything I can for, be there for me? I am still in the force, but I feel that I'm a civilian again. It has taken my pride in my uniform from me. My car I have looked after so well, I can no longer drive for over 10 to 15 miles without wanting to sleep. I'm hanging on the edge of a cliff about to go over and it doesn't matter. It's like they have left me to jump and drown with a ton of bricks in my arms.

There are leaflets all over the police station for suicide, saying 'Talk to me'. They tell you to talk, do this, do that, but then when you do, no one wants to respond. I went on a training course for the police motorcycle outriders. VIPEX they call it. It's the training needed to be an outrider to escort the Queen or Prime Minister. I passed the initial course but failed the refresher because I wasn't thinking straight. I remember I put a tweet out thanking the West Yorkshire Police for understanding I was having issues. It was the first thing I had ever failed, and I pointed out that I would be back and smash it when I was well. Hashtag mental health. What happened next was something that shocked and destroyed my confidence. Got to work Monday morning and they pull all my permits. They thought me to be mentally unstable. That came from a tweet, a police tweet. How can I be mentally unstable for writing a tweet? The powers that be didn't like that I had put a mental health tweet out. No one spoke to me before they took the action, and that cannot be right. It was a tweet, just a tweet.

All the posters and labels around the station saying, 'please talk to us' meant nothing. All I have done is try to talk and got slaughtered for it. What message does that send? It tells you not to talk to anyone, look at Ben to see the repercussions of trusting the organisation to be there to support you. Months later I was having the piss taken out of me in the office for tweeting and hash tagging mental health. The stigma will always remain with me.

I don't want it to appear that no one supported me. My inspector and my sergeant were sympathetic and brilliant. They called, texted, and visited me. No one else bothered, and I believe that the institution washed its hands of me immediately. I was told to stop using the police twitter and not put anything on it whilst I was ill. I was told it was not a good look. People would wonder about my absence. I felt lost, left out. I was hurting. Phone calls I was making to find out what my situation was went unanswered. I was feeling let down by the people I had served loyally for 19 years. The same people who had praised me for the work I had done and commended me putting me forward for awards.

If I were to sum up my thoughts, I would say that they saw me as a high-profile bobby. They didn't know what to do with me, so passed the buck around in the hope I would disappear. Become forgotten. I was a number on a piece of paper, a number they wanted to forget. I don't think the organisation knows what to do with someone who isn't fitting into the blue blocks anymore. My blue blocks were disintegrating before their eyes and they didn't know how to cope with it.

If someone comes along and says. 'I'm gender neutral, don't classify me as a female or male officer.' Or someone doesn't use certain toilets because of their religion. What would they do? They would act quickly to rectify the issue. Everything would trigger. As an institution they understand the need for a person to have different values and beliefs and will go all out to meet their needs, but they have not understood the needs of someone with mental health problems. The banners and posters may be up, but none of them know what to do for that person once a cry for help goes out. They would be like, 'fuck me, he's cried out.... now what? There's nothing in the manual'.

What needs understanding is that response officers have little control over their day-to-day activity. It's the nature of the role. You cannot plan your day. There can be periods of high-octane incidents where the public is angry and upset. Dealing with those who have witnessed an incident is stressful. Shift work burns you out, your sleeping pattern is all over the place and effects a normal social life so isolation can result. Add to that the high expectations that someone who is the victim of crime, has in the police, puts immense emotional distress on you to live up to that standard. This isn't something new, it's well known in the force. Why hide the emotional damage to officers? That is what I find hard to grasp.

There appears to be no infrastructure to help a mentally ill officer. My brain doesn't work normally anymore. I'm ill and I'm crying out. If a thought tells me to do something or not do something, I could listen to it. It could tell me to go jump off a cliff, cut your wrists, step out in front of a car. Your brain doesn't get the value of. 'You can wait three weeks for an appointment.' It doesn't happen like that. If I attend a domestic and a guy with a knife threatening to cut himself. I would ring the crisis team and they would deal with it immediately because he has a mental health issue. I'm not offered the same respect. I feel that if you are wearing a uniform, they expect you to wait. The paper trail gets longer and longer, and the waiting time expands.

Another example that upsets me greatly. The Police applied for my medical records from my doctor. The Surgery asked them to pay £130 pounds for access. Right or wrong, that is the charge a doctor makes. West Yorkshire police didn't pay promptly, so the police doctors are waiting to get the report. My doctor is waiting for payment and I must wait for them all before I can get a psychiatrist appointment to carry out a full assessment. Am I angry, wouldn't you be? The only resolution was that I pay whilst waiting.

On the Home Front

To be open and talk about the effects of my decline into mental illness with brutal honesty is hard. That difficulty increases tenfold when I think about the effects it has had on my family and especially my partner Milly. We met at work and I am so grateful she is a fellow officer. Her understanding of the job goes without saying. The benefit of her knowledge has enabled her to become the rock I so desperately needed.

HANDCUFFED EMOTIONS

It was back in 2009. I was in the canteen, and I noticed this blonde girl eating a sandwich. I remember laughing at the smallness of her feet. So small, her trousers covered them. I had just come out of a relationship so didn't really want to start another. That meant that we became good friends long before beginning a relationship. We enjoyed each other's company, then they put Milly as my oppo a few times so she would be out on the job with me, seeing and experiencing the same as I was. Milly was, and is, a beat cop, but there are always opportunities arising to allow police officers to see what others do. Milly used to volunteer to come out with the traffic cops.

Vanity is a strange thing that we carry within us. It means we enjoy being told why someone likes us. It was a question I asked Milly. Her answer. 'I like your sense of humour; you make me laugh.' It was a trait that appealed to her. That was an appropriate description of me back then. Both of us were very cagey at first. Police are notorious for internal affairs and we didn't want anyone to know about our relationship. I suspect they guessed, but if they did, no one said anything. To us, the lack of gossip was a blessing. Being private people, it was something we could do without.

Aware that the jobs I went to involved fatal accidents. Something that, like other officers, I dealt with. Milly was used to me going home, having a beer, and going to bed. She knew that at work they expected me to carry on as normal. To cope with all I witnessed, no matter what that was without support. That was the expectation. The team might ask you if you were okay, but the common answer would always be Yes! You had an image to think about and as a copper she knew fully that no one wanted to be the one who 'lost it'.

Milly always says to me she knew I was changing. She saw it, following the high-speed chase where the lad had his legs crushed. He was the one sitting innocently on a wall, legs dangling down. Aware that knowing I was being investigated for my driving was causing me stress. Only Milly saw that, and it upset her. Telling me I wasn't responsible for the lad's injuries meant nothing in my confused brain. She knew it had torn me apart. Milly had also been called to the scene and gave the lad first aid, holding his hand as he lay screaming at her to help him. What she didn't know was that I was the officer driving the pursuit car. They only told her they had taken me away once they had removed the victim from the scene.

HANDCUFFED EMOTIONS

Milly was unaware if they had taken me for questioning about the accident, or something else, but she was told she needed to stay away from me. Investigation issues were the reason given. To tell her that was hard when she knew I needed her. She knew me better than anyone and told me it hurt her, knowing she had to obey orders. She knew I would be distraught and devastated and torn inside being investigated for the horrific injuries of a young man. They let her see me some hours later, and she always says that it was like it had turned my world upside down. I was questioning myself repeatedly. Had I made the right decision? Could I have done something differently? Milly was just as relieved as I was when they found I had done nothing wrong. That said, she is more than aware I still blame myself. When I asked to see the male, it pleased her to learn he did not hold responsible.

I used to tell her my view on driving had changed once we had our daughter. She was my world, and I idolised her. I slowed down. I needed to come home at night. I had a family. Whenever you have children in the police force, your life changes. You become more aware of the dangers. More alert to the nutter with a knife or gun. Unfortunately, you become more emotionally astute when you are dealing with incidents involving children. If they are a similar age to your own, you go home and start drilling road safety into your kids. Milly recognises that I do this a lot.

My illness has made me paranoid about the dangers of running into roads. I know the speed that idiots drive at and the consequences if it hits a child. I think every parent should teach their children about road safety, let alone allow them out late at night. It takes me back to an incident that appeared on Police Interceptors. I was in Bingley; it was 1.30 am. A boy who has stolen a vehicle was driving around the local area like a maniac. When he was seen, he made off at speed and I pursued him. He was boxed in after being stung and we apprehended him. He turned out to be 12 years old. What is a child of that age doing out, never mind driving a car?

The incident that occurred in 2016, Milly remembers well. I have talked about it so often with her and, as I have already stated, it is the stuff that my nightmares are based on. That was the little boy run over by the truck. I know I have mentioned this several times, but so great was the impact on me my memoir warrants it. Milly has told me things about that day I have forgotten. She recalls me ringing her, to say that I would be late. Nothing unusual about this, but she noticed that I sounded upset. With the serious of the incident, she didn't feel this was abnormal. Then I got home and burst into tears. It appalled her to know they had sent me back to do paperwork and not asked if I was all right.

Milly watched as I continued to go to work. Continued to deal with multiple accidents. Fatal road traffic collisions and horrific injuries. Torn inside, she tried to do everything she could to understand what I was experiencing in my head. Aware my dad was dying and how close to him I was. She always laughed and said I hadn't cut the apron string. It was a standing joke. Knowing our closeness, she stood by me in every way she could. We talked about my fear that I was next in line and supported me during the two months I had to take off work with depression.

Milly realised how, when I returned to work, I was finding it harder and harder to go. She was living through all of this with me. She watched as I got increasingly tired and withdrew into myself. I wanted to be at home, safe with my family. I realise how hard this had to be for her. The knowledge that she was still out on the beat, still experiencing her own traumas day in, day out, filled me with fear for her. Being diagnosed with depression and anxiety gave her some hope that I would recover and be all right. The harder I found everyday living, the harder she found it.

When my chest got tight and I thought I was having a heart attack, Milly shared my fear. She became my safety blanket, and I didn't want her to go to work and leave me. The strain on her was growing, and I knew it. In 2011, my short-term memory was damaged. This was following the brain injury I suffered in a crash. We have talked about her feelings when she came to the hospital and saw me on a stretcher. They taped me down with blocks around my head. It scared her when I was trying to speak to her but couldn't. I had developed a stutter. In her words, she recognised that it had left me with major confidence issues. I also developed a dribble and didn't want people to see me.

On top of her own job, she became my memory, writing things down to remind me when I had speech therapy. A woman came who specialised in showing her how to help me recover my memory. I was in a position where I wouldn't speak to people because the incident had affected my speech. Milly will say that I still have memory issues now. She feels these have got worse since last year. I am becoming more reliant on her to remind me of things. Make notes for me. I joke with her; she is my walking calendar. Simple things like taking the kids to school and picking them back up. She must remind me to do it on time. I know it's draining for her.

It became obvious to Milly that I was really struggling when I didn't want to go to work. She watched me sit in my car and find it hard to breathe. Commented on the way I was sweating. Knew I wasn't sleeping and that my nightmares were crippling me. As a family, we were becoming detached from friends because of me. In August 2019, she went to work, and I rang her upset. She told me she thought I was suffering from PTSD. Milly had been doing some research to understand what I was experiencing. Recognising that my symptoms fit the criteria. The way I had seen the little boy as being my daughter. Freezing at the spot. All of which she said were classic of the illness.

I know that all police officers have certain jobs which remain with them. Some good, some bad. Little things remind them, like driving past the same road on which an accident occurred. With me, though, it went beyond that. Milly could see that I physically froze when passing somewhere that reminded me of a fatal. I was thankful that she wasn't there on the day I was out for a walk with the kids and a police siren went off. I couldn't move, I literally wet myself. It filled me with fear and immediately set me re-living my own experiences.

I have everything to thank Milly for; she was the first one to recognise that I could have PTSD. 'Seek help, you need it.' She insisted and made me an appointment. All this was taking place with the added burden of making sure the kids remained unaware of my illness. They are young and you want their memories of dad to be wonderful memories. To them daddy is a policeman, and he has a poorly head. They don't question why I am at home. As a shift worker, it is easy to explain it away by saying it's my off days. All they see is daddy is on TV, daddy gets recognised by people in the street. He has his picture taken and plays with them.

I don't let them see me when I am at my worst. In the same way, we don't tell them the ins and outs of policing. To them, mummy and daddy get the evil men. They will innocently ask how many bad men we caught that day. It's important to us both that we protect them from what we really do. The reality is too gruesome. Police children must be resilient. They learn that might be home late. That there are no regular times they will see you. You may miss their birthdays, Xmas, or holidays. We may not get away to see school plays or go to open days. If a big event happens, we must be there. It's the job. These facts they take in their stride.

A normal Monday to Friday, nine to five working life is not something they have. There are colleagues who hand their children over in the carpark as they exchange shifts with each other. All that matters to them is who is getting up in the morning or putting them to bed. Making sure that one or the other is home to do this becomes important for us both. Providing a routine is vital for them to develop normally. The changes in me have placed a lot of this burden on Milly. As she tries to keep as much normality as she can amidst coping with my changing moods.

I know she finds it exhausting. To her, I have become a third child she has to care for. Making sure I attend appointments and know what I am supposed to be doing and when. She constantly must think for two people. Get up early with the kids to take the pressure from me so I can try to sleep. The most fearful thing Milly faces is not knowing if it will ever go back to how it was. It has been going on so long now that it's hard to remember how it was. We both agree that we are living a new normal. She frets when I stress over things, out of my control. Worries, will they pension me off or not? How will we manage? The uncertainty of not knowing if I will be paid or not, adds to the pressure. These are the things that people do not see or associate with mental illness.

Milly didn't know me before I joined the police. It is the only image she has seen of me. What she knows is that I am no longer the man she met eleven years ago. Seeing me go from a happy, funny, outgoing person to a man who no longer feels anything and cannot express himself anymore. Someone who is numb. Externally, people may still see me as the happy cheeky chappy. That is the front I put on. Only Milly knows that beneath the mask I am broken.

I don't think anyone, but Milly could understand my illness in the way she does. If I am crying or upset, she is there because she knows the dimensions of the job. What it takes to be a police officer. Even though I think there are downsides to being with a partner in the same job as you, there are advantages. I don't have to explain to her what I've seen and why I have become ill, Milly knows. Any person whose partner is a bobby knows how difficult it can be. There is no such thing as a normal weekend or normal day. It all adds to the stress.

From my point of view, I could see that Milly was suffering. I see her in pain, watching me. We talked about a lot and it wasn't easy. I know the way I was with our son cut her up. The most painful part was that she knew I much I wanted a boy. She tried to understand why I felt such fear at the thought of hurting him or holding him, but it was hard for her. I didn't even realise how much I had detached myself from him. I have this awful feeling that I left him behind. I know I didn't, but my illness does strange things to my mind.

Milly looks at me when I drill into them not to go onto the road, sometimes, they cry. My message is so strong. I feel ashamed that I have not been the dad I should have been. They are brilliant kids, but I breed it into them where they can and cannot go. We have a rule and my kids are more than aware of it. 'If I go down there, daddy can't see me so he can't protect me.' If my daughter is on her bike, I must always be able to see her.

I will never understand it when I see kids out on the streets at 9 pm. Little children no older than three or four years. It takes a second for a white van to pull up and they're gone. I know it comes back to the little boy under the truck. He had ridden into the path of a truck on a little bike. I would hope that would never happen to my kids. I would rather be overprotective than not give a shit where they are or what they are doing. I know if it wasn't for my family, I wouldn't be here now. I would have topped myself.

So much has happened to me. I always ask Milly if I have been a good dad. I know before all of this I was a wonderful dad. As my illness deepened, I can't say I was the best dad. I wasn't the dad they saw as a play dad. Dad, who's there to wrestle with them. Powerful dad. Let's go out somewhere dad. I'm not always aware of how my illness is affecting how I am with them, but I know that I do everything I can to give them normality. I smile at when I took them down to the local pub garden. I had rung up and been told no one was in, so off we went. It has a big bowling green so they could run all over. They loved it. Dad was taking them out.

Even though I feel a numbness and I know I don't show love in the same way. I know I love my kids and Milly. Do I wish this hadn't happened to me? I do, but it has, and I must live in hope I can get better. Hoping I can be there for my family and they will forgive me for the times of stress and pain I have put them through. I hope I can regain my feeling for life and make up for all the bad times. There is a saying that when you are 20 you fall and bounce back. At 30 you bounce and crack, but by 40 you bounce, break and struggle to get back up. That's how I feel. I have bounced, broken, and I'm struggling to find my way back.

Coping with PTSD

Knowing that I have an illness described as long term and life changing compounds the fear I already feel. There are two types of PTSD. They call the one I am suffering with Complex PTSD or C-PTSD. Interestingly, the Equal Equality Act of 2010 states that a mental health condition is a disability when it influences normal activity. It does not recognise PTSD as one condition fitting this category. Yet, they see it to be a debilitating illness that changes the life of the sufferer. I don't understand that at all.

HANDCUFFED EMOTIONS

C-PTSD is the repeated exposure to traumatic events. They give the symptoms as disassociation, chest pains, emotional loss of control causing numbness of feelings. Physical distress including nausea, sweating, rapid heart rate. These I experience along with flashbacks, nightmares, and a loss of interest in life and daily activities. I feel a failure and worthless. I'm not leading a normal life and I don't know if I ever will again.

Since diagnosis I have done some research on my condition. What I read does not make me confident of recovery in the short term. I realise now that I have had a psychological reaction to the traumatic events I have witnessed over a long period. This accounts for the feelings I have had for a long time that something wasn't right with me. Some see depression as an add on to C-PTSD, others see it as part of the condition. Trust becomes a question mark so when you reach out and they betray you for doing so, trust depletes even further.

I am trying to understand my illness, to enable me to cope better with the symptoms. I know my self-perception has changed. I know I'm different and it makes me ashamed. There has been a change in my relationships. I am seeking a rescuer, someone to take me out of this. There has been a loss of meaning in my core beliefs that affects my hope in the World itself. My understanding of life has become distorted. It didn't surprise me to find out that what the experts consider as traumatic situations include, serious road accidents, violent assaults, and personal loss. My job provided the first two, my parent's death, the latter.

Most people associate PTSD with the armed forces, soldiers and those who are on the battlefield. It is common to see veterans suffering from the condition and accepted. We are aware and understood that what they have experienced. We see it on the news and TV. What police officers go through is less well known. It's the same with organisations such as the ambulance and fire services. The everyday services which deal with dangerous situations every working day. How many dead bodies can you see or mangled car crash victims before it affects you? Most people face some trauma in their lifetime, but usually the time lag is lengthy between them. It gives them time to heal and recover. That isn't the case with traffic cops.

One of my worst fears is that I have no identity or purpose left. I feel like I'm in a prison cell; the door is open, but I don't know how to get out. My path in life has disappeared. It has come to its end. I'm scared of losing my home, Milly, and my kids. I don't feel good enough for them. My page is now blank. I'm broken as a person. They have let me down and I feel I'm owed an explanation. I have lost the camaraderie I had at work. I'm not one of the team anymore. My dream job has become my nightmare. I have lost friends and there is a big void where Ben used to be.

The positive side of living with PTSD and not being able to work is that I get more time to see my kids. I may not feel the emotion of love, but I feel touch when they hug me. I have the memory of my little boy kissing my cheek and I get to see them grow up. I may be a poorly dad, but I'm a dad. They know I'm ill. My daughter went to school and told her teacher that dad is poorly, he's got a poorly head. He's seen a lot of bad things at work, so he can't work anymore. How innocent and loving is that? Their funny ways and their laughter I love. I missed much of that before my illness took hold.

A weight has lifted from my shoulders, I don't have to dread going out to work. I no longer need to run towards trouble. I don't work shifts anymore. I can do simple things like cut the grass or wash the car. The blue boxes that once filled my body are breaking down. Replaced by C-PTSD symptoms that fill not only my body but also my mind. I would still be there if anyone needed my help, but I would turn the other way if I saw a thief running from a shop.

I find it strange when people say. 'I'm sorry this has happened to you; how do you feel?' What do I tell them? 'Well, here is how I truly feel. I'm a failure, I'm weakened. I don't like what I see in the mirror. I hate who I have become. I don't deserve what has happened to me. I don't have the support I need. I feel betrayed. Most of all, I can't deal with you.' Instead, I tell them I'm coping. I'll get well again. What am I expected to say?' I'm at home a lot, it's hard. I've had something taken from me.

When you first start out you have a path mapped out. You want a career, get married, have kids, a nice car and house. Your purpose is strong, you know where you are going. You want to travel the world; these are the ambitions they teach us to esteem to. Now, I feel I'm not good enough to carry on. I'm a 44-year-old, I've got a mortgage and I'm shit scared. I don't see myself as an officer anymore. If I look at the positive of that, I don't have to be someone I'm not. I don't have to hide away, and I'm not scared to tell people I'm ill. I know there are fewer people in my life now. I don't think anyone will invite me to the Christmas party. I'm broken, it's all I can repeat.

Can I mend? I hope so. Knowing I'm not going back to a job I loved is more than hard. I'm no longer a teammate or a Bobby. I've become another person they know, but not the one they knew as a police officer. I have a big void, but real friends in the force will still be friends, otherwise they won't be worth worrying about. I may be still ill, but I appreciate life a lot more now. I enjoy feeling the sun on my face. So even though I know I'm damaged it doesn't stop me wanting to get well. I may not like myself, but I like things around me now.

It a challenging time, 2020 with Covid 19 hasn't made things easier, but that's true for all of us. Things are closed, but it gives the opportunity to enjoy the basic things life offers. To take a walk, be outside, simple activities. I'm on a learning journey now, every page I turn is blank, and it's up to me to fill it. Does that scare the shit out of me, you bet it does? I've always tried to put 100% in everything I do. Tried to succeed. Be at the top of my game. Right from the start. Green Keeping, tiling, motorbike sales, police. I've always strived to be the best

I can be. Now I must see how far the learning curve will extend and the journey will take me.

Just recognising the number of sufferers affected by PTSD or mental illness has amazed me. I remember putting out a tweet; it got 8300 likes, 766 comments and was interacted with 554,000 times. There are people out there who are poorly. Part of my coping is knowing that I can put my story out there and they see the similarities in their own symptoms. It helps them, and it helps me. I feel good being able to voice my experiences. I may not want to face people yet, but I'm comfortable writing my stuff down. If I meet someone from work, my stomach still tightens up and I can't express myself as I want to. People at work don't really ask about my condition because they don't know how to deal with it, so it makes me reluctant to talk with them.

Writing this book gives me a sense of achievement. I have always been interested in the stories told about my father and grandfather. I want to leave something my own children will look at and say, 'That's our dad's book. He went through a lot, but he never gave up hope.' Talking about things is important, and I see that now. I go to the pub with mates, but it's different.

HANDCUFFED EMOTIONS

You don't want to go into a four-hour conversation about PTSD but to talk with someone that I'm comfortable with, really helps me. What I really want in life is not to be a millionaire, I don't want to be famous, but I want to help people. I always loved tutoring trainees on the job. So irrespective, if only one person picked up and read this book and said that it impacted on them. That it had made them open to talking about their suffering and they now know they are not alone in this. What more could I want?

If somebody from West Yorkshire Police reads this, I want them to know that they didn't do enough for me and they don't do enough to protect their own when it comes down to the line. This illness affects people more than they will ever realise. Even though they have failed me, I hope my story helps them to find suitable ways to care for their employee's mental health. After all, without the frontline staff, who will protect the community? They could have done much more for officers with mental illness. Just read this and realise that people are not machines, they are men and women in uniform. When they cry out for help, you have a duty of care that any employer has. I want them to know how hard it is for me, an Action Jackson, one elite, the guy on telly, to come out and say, I need help. It really hurts, more than anyone can know. To make that decision to bare my soul. To tell people I cry every night.

I know it's all right to cry. I wouldn't do it on a bus, but I no longer think I'm not a man if I show my emotions. I want those who read this book to know that. It doesn't matter if they work at Morrisons, are a doctor or driver. If they want to cry, then cry. It cleanses the soul and gets rid of a lot of demons, Milly laughs at me when I say that. She recalls the times I would watch something on TV and say, 'Look at that wet lettuce.' When they got tearful. I now admire people who are not afraid to show their feelings.

It's strange living with PTSD, I can't say it's not, but I am learning to cope. I have a concern now that Milly is still in the force but in the same way that I chose my career, so did she. I would never put pressure on her to change what she enjoys doing. The noticeable difference, whereas before we would have openly talked about the day's events, now, if Milly has attended a fatal, she doesn't tell me about it. We still talk about the light-hearted stuff, silly things that go on. It's a big part of her life and we can't just ignore that.

HANDCUFFED EMOTIONS

What do I feel about her job? The police are a very cliquey organisation. A lot of tittle-tattle about things. Can Milly handle it? Yes, she can. Do I get bothered that she is out working nights when I'm home in bed, no. She has always done it. Could she get hurt? That worries me, but I know she understands the job and is careful. We have always had this pact that if any of us gets a phone call in the night to say the other is injured and is in hospital, unless it's life or death. You stay with the kids. We do not leave the kids unless it's fatal. That's the way you must compromise as a police officer whose partner is also an officer. You go back to bed and sort it in the morning. No panic, no rash decisions.

Sometimes a colleague has driven my car home. Milly opens the door, asks where I am. It's usually in casualty because of an injury and I'm on ward 15. It's the life we have lived, now I know that will change. I will be the one on the receiving end of such late-night calls. Will I be able to handle it? I will, when you have been in that life you understand it. Imagine now you as you read this book. How often do you get a call at 4am to say your partner has been in a car crash?

BENJAMIN PEARSON

They have a broken arm, and a fractured leg. Do you panic, grab the kids, and rush off? If it happens once, maybe. If it's a frequent episode, you need a routine for dealing with it. The important thing is to keep the kids stable. Give them as normal a life as is possible.

If I go back to the question of fear. I am afraid that Milly will become like me. That the job will break her. She has 13 years' service in and although there are a lot of bad things she has seen; they haven't been in the category of those I have endured. If she ever decides to come out of the force, I'll support her. Whatever her decision is, I'll be there for her as she is there for me. I can't ask anymore of her than I have already asked. Milly has given up everything for my illness and I just want her to be happy. I'm cynical now. If it comes down on her and she cracks, I'll just say, I'm here.

I'm proud of Milly more than I can say. She puts up with my nightmares, my down times and still tried all she can to get me to laugh, to enjoy family events. Keep things organised, hold us all together. Keep me together, she's like superglue and I love her for it. There are many living with PTSD who do not have that support. Poorly people ostracised by society, who end up on the streets. It's not their fault, It's the cruelty of the mind, the manipulation of the senses.

You cannot control the way you will be from day to day. Concentration on coping with it is all you have. There is no cure for PTSD.

The Healing Process

I was told that I would need some intervention to help me through the healing process. Some of it I would find hard. I would have to re-live my experiences, examine them to view them differently. The focus of the treatment is therapy alongside medications, which is to help me change my negative behaviours, thoughts, and feelings by re-framing the traumas I have seen. This then helps me to deal with them and learn healthy ways of coping. It wasn't an idea that appealed to me. I knew I would have to face my nightmares. Expose myself to hard memories that I wanted to avoid, but to me, it wasn't a choice. I want desperately to gain control over my life again. Get my self-identity back and be able to stop being the poor guy with C-PTSD.

My interventions started with me being sent to the Mental Health Unit in Shipley several times. I've had constant assessments, repeatedly, each lasting one hour. I can't lie, my first thought when I looked around at the people there was, I don't belong here. Then as I sat there waiting, it hit me I was one of them. They were going through their own mental illnesses in the same way I was. Every one of us trying to find ourselves again.

The doctor and the police force were trying to arrange various appointments. It became confusing who was doing what and when. I was also becoming increasingly stressed at the lack of any actual movement. The assessments left me crying, upset, and feeling worthless. They passed me, like a ball, from one therapist to another because of the complexity of my illness. I was told by one therapist that I was too complicated to deal with. I had already faced five sessions with Red Arc, an independent charity, after mum died, but it was just talking about how I felt on a day to day basis.

I was then told I could go through the Police Federation and they arranged six sessions with Socrates in Huddersfield. There I would see more therapists. The first three or four I was in tears; it was so tiring. It shattered me by the time I got to the end of the session. I wasn't sure what was going on and it was an hour and half journey to get there and the same back. By the time I got home, I had nothing left in me.

I don't know what I expected. Maybe I had watched too many television programmes. The type where you lie on a big black couch and the conversation goes along like. 'So, tell me about your childhood, what your parents did to you.' Or 'I will regress you and start at the beginning.' I did not understand was the truth. What I got was. 'So, how are you doing? Okay then, I'll see you next you week.' I was there spilling my guts, baring my soul, and I seemed to get nothing back from it.

I was told that what they are doing is trying to get you to empty yourself. Rid you of the negative thoughts and emotions. Getting to know who you are and getting you to open the door. The problem is, you can't get through a lot in an hour. As quick as they started, the six sessions were over. What's the benefit of that? Then you find out it isn't free, technically, it's coming out of your wage. Well, hang on a minute! Thankfully, by that time, the NHS had seen me through my doctor and recognised how damaged I was. They took me on as long-term permanent care.

This has been different because Paul, who I'm seeing now, is nice, but I find the therapy strange. He talks to me about your mind becoming your friend. Is it being nice to you today? Is it helping you today? I never thought about my mind in that way until he explains the theories behind it. He also tells me what videos would be good for me to watch. I feel that when I'm having therapy it isn't so much about me opening up, which is what I do. It's about him really stripping it back. I am challenged because he will stop me and explore what I've just said. Questioning what I mean.

I have developed a habit of saying sorry when I've done nothing to be sorry for. What makes me say sorry all the time and why I do that, my therapist has explained to me. The sessions have brought out a lot of stuff in me. We were just moving onto EMDR when the lock down came. EMDR stands for Eye Movement Desensitisation Reprocessing where the therapist directs my eye movements to help me process my traumatic memories. The process attempts to take the focus off the event by diverting my attention and distracting me. It is to take away my psychological stress and will hopefully be helpful.

It's a longer-term therapy and has different phases. Starting with my history, the first phase tests are where I am and where I need to be. It then moves to the next stage that aims to teach me coping strategies. Stage three is the assessment part taking me to phases 4, 5, 6 and 7 where the EMDR techniques are used to target specific memories. As I understand it, these stages are the hardest because it will force me to face my demons. The last part is testing my progress. I'm not too sure what to tell you, as you read this. Is it successful? I don't know because we had only just ramped up my therapy when Covid 19 struck.

I have had EMDR since November but only the first stages, so I haven't been able to start the full process. It hasn't been good because they won't allow them to do this using Zoom, and I can only speak to my therapist over the phone. They have got no dates yet to go back, so I'm stuck. We spend an hour once a week speaking to each other. It is really frustrating for me and Paul, my therapist.

I ask myself if I have seen any improvement and I can say that I haven't seen improvements in sleeping, but I have improved the way I look at myself. I can sit and know if my mind is being my friend and now, I know what's wrong with me, I can understand when I'm not feeling well. I now know it's all right to challenge myself, to say, 'no, I can't do it.' If I don't feel like doing something. If Milly asks me to go out with her and the kids, I can say, no. I don't have to feel guilty about that. I don't have to justify myself. I can control what I do. If I know I need a snooze, then I can have one.

I have also tried to do things again that I used to do before. Activities like running, but the difference is that if I can only run a mile, I don't have to feel a failure. I can say, I have done well for trying. It's okay not to do things I can't do anymore. My mate Dov, a Fire Fighter at Bingley, does a 100-mile run over a few days, but I don't feel bad because I can't do that. 'Don't worry about what others feel or whether they are judging you'.

Am I fixed? No, I'm nowhere near being fixed, but I have come a long way since the start. I think I would be a lot further forward if it weren't for Covid. I only sleep for three to four hours each night. I cry all the time. I'm distant from most of the people I know because of my horrendous outbreaks of disassociation. I am open-minded about therapy and I'm pleased I am having it. I would more than recommend it to anyone with a mental illness. What is there to lose?

Anti-depression tablets are part of my life now. For how long I don't know, but I don't see it as a stigma anymore. Part way through, I also had to sit through a two-and-a-half-hour session with an independent psychiatrist arranged through work. They wanted to assess whether I will ever be fit enough to return to the service. One of her recommendations was that I would enjoy a concoction of medications to help with my illness alongside the one I already take. I accept this because I know I need that now, but I don't want to be one of those who goes through an airport with a plastic bag full of pills. I must then explain to someone who will think I'm nuts.

The zoom session I endured with her was an horrendous experience. I wept for the entire session. I had to go through my childhood right up to the support I had at home. She asked me how things were at work, what led up to my illness. The questions went on and on. Raking up things from my past and present. She concluded that it began with the bump I had at work in 2011 where I had to have the speech therapy. It all started from that point there which I had never associated with it. It was then that negative things kicked into my psyche.

Her report says I won't be fit for work for another 12 to 18 months and then it's unlikely I will ever be able to go back into the police force. If I remain on the same path as I am on now with my therapy and support structure. Provided I have no setbacks, I should be able to return to some form of work but not traumatic work. I would then have to see if I could sustain working. I should eventually be fit to go back, but whether that will be part-time or full-time I don't know yet. I'm not at that stage, so can't say.

Her recommendation is that I am not fit to be a Bobby anymore and I must leave the police. Part of me is pleased with that. I have a friend who was a Bobby. The same happened to him and he said that he didn't really feel well again until he was out of the force and back into normal life. Only then did he feel whole and put the police and his experiences behind him. I hope that happens to me.

They have classed me as severe C-PTSD, severe depression, all work related and aspirated by losing my parents closely together. The official diagnosis didn't surprise me, but it made me feel different. The interview wrecked me totally. It shattered me and I still feel the effects of it on my mental state. At least now I understand what has happened to me. In all my 19 years on the force I have had no training about PTSD, I have seen nothing put into place to support sufferers so when it happens you are in limbo. You think you are going mad and can't see a reason for it.

With therapy, I felt more on a plateau than I did. Yes, I'm aware I'm ill, but now when I feel a downward spiral coming, I understand it. I feel my whole body starting to ache days before. I become withdrawn from the World. If you haven't experienced PTSD, you cannot understand this. I know there are those who comment I'm enjoying lazing about home. They think you are blagging it. They have little idea of my life. My illness has taken me over, day, and night. I feel everything is passing me by. I'm stood on a train platform, but I can't get on the train.

I take sleeping tablets just to get me into night-time mode. They shut me down from the pressures of half pay and the time the process is taking. Do they work? Partly, but nothing has been successful in stopping the nightmares yet.

BENJAMIN PEARSON

A Commended Officer

When I am feeling down, I sit and look back on the good aspects of my career in the West Yorkshire Police Force. I look at the certificates on my wall. Eight Divisional Commendations for which I am proud. Four awarded for bravery, four for fighting crime and denying criminals the run of the road. Three Judges recommendations, one of which is for the arrest of a murderer in R vs Swinbank. One for the impact of my arrests on crime and the final one I received for pulling four burglary suspects out of a crashed stolen car on fire.

Reading the examples in my PDP and the many letters and emails of thanks from the public, brings me some peace. The worth of such positive recognition, any Police Officer will value highly. I value it greatly. It justifies the work I do and promotes a pride in myself when I look back. To most people, receiving an award is a tremendous achievement. It tells you and others that you have not only gone above and beyond the call of duty, but you have been recognised for it by senior officers or the public at large. To a police officer, it's especially important. Coppers never really get any thanks for putting their lives on the line, so when you do, you carry it with you. It means the world.

I can't remember the order of the commendations I have received; all are of equal importance to me, but the letters of thanks from those I have directly helped are special. They come from the heart. It blows you away. They express their thanks that when they were not there in a loved one's hour of need, they knew that you were. You know that it is you they will remember for your kindness for the rest of their lives. They make all the times I am called 'Knob head, wanker, prick and piggy bastard' sink into oblivion. When it matters, the public at large know and acknowledge I have done a good job. PTSD makes you question that over and over.

I keep every letter and thank you email that I have received, and they will remain with me as much as the memories of the events they relate to. My heartfelt thanks go out to all of those who cared enough to write to me. In a strange way, you, without knowing it, are helping now in my healing.

Looking at the commendations on my wall does often take me back. One of the more humorous entries in my PDP for example, was when an old man had stolen a car down South and used it to visit his brother. It was raining, and we got him out of the rain whilst we investigated. Wrong as it was to steal a car, he got to see his brother before being caught. That was way back in 2006, I was still a rookie learning the ropes, but I received thanks from his family for looking after him.

Another comment that has importance for me is a general report and reads:

Ben, thank you for the hard work you did last year. You need to think positively about times ahead and recognise your strengths. Your performance is high. The way you come across and the impression you leave is good. You are committed and professional. Your culture is right. Nothing is beyond your remit and you are viewed as a team player and are completely omni competent.

It continues in the same vein and I don't expect someone reading this book to understand, as much as I do, what it means to me. It reminds me I was once exceptionally good at my job and recognised as having a commendable attitude.

The next comment shows a similarity between the incident that tipped me over the edge and the way as 'ill' Ben I reacted to it and the difference in my reactions as' well' Ben to an incident that occurred some years ago. The comments read:

Ben, we have discussed the stressful environment encountered at this Fatal RTC the other day. The tragic circumstances that involved the death of a small child. For your part you were consummately professional in your handling of the control of the early stages. You performed admirably…….. Take credit for your professionalism and human compassion showed in relation to the incident.

A lot of the reports relate to the pursuit and apprehension of criminals. As a traffic cop, it is everyday bread and butter to me. Re-reading them is still therapeutic for me and gives me back a glimpse of the pride I have lost in myself. A step above the Personal reports are my actual commendation certificates, displayed in frames on my wall. A reminder of the good times when I was one of the lads. Had all my blue cubes in their place and was respected for the role I played.

A memorable Keighley Divisional Award they put me forward for came about after an incident involving a man wielding a knife. I was still a beat bobby then and on patrol when I saw a man who was acting strangely. I was tutoring a probationer at the time who had only been with me one week, so I had a responsibility to safeguard my trainee and deal with the situation. I moved closer to the man and saw he had a knife and seemed agitated. It was a dangerous situation and could have turned bad quickly.

I called in the situation to my colleagues and set about controlling the incident. The man then walked towards the Town centre, holding the 7" blade to his own throat. Things were becoming potentially volatile. To allow time for a shield team to intervene, I talked to the guy to build some rapport with him. By this time public interest was being aroused. When that happens first thing on your mind is protect the public and the inexperienced probationer, so I used my vehicle as a blockade.

My attention then turned fully to the guy wielding the knife. It was clear he wasn't acting normal and had some mental disorder. The more officers that arrived on the scene, the more he threatened to take his life. I was trying to calm him and gain his trust. I put my baton and belt down to reassure him I would not harm him. He then moved towards me and got to within feet before he bent down and placed his knife on the floor. They awarded me a Divisional Commander's Certificate of Merit for my handling of the situation.

I found out later that he had a long history of mental illness. After the incident, they sectioned him. Strange that I helped him then without fully understanding his mental state. I see it now. They ran the story in the newspaper. They called me a hero. I wasn't a hero; I just did my job to the best of my ability. Police Officers don't see themselves as heroes. They see themselves as trained specialists whose sole purpose is to protect the public, safeguard other officers and take control of any situation that arises. No more, no less.

BENJAMIN PEARSON

The newspaper article was the first of many. Like most things, the first one is always the one you have fond memories of. It's always a strange experience to see yourself pasted across newspapers, but it's also a great feeling. Your teammates know what you have done, and they are extremely proud of you. They also take the piss out of you weeks after. I came in work nearly every day to find my image taped to my tray with graffiti of every type drawn over my face. It's all in fun and part of the team banter. Do I miss it. You bet I do. Will I ever get it back, be part of that banter in another workplace? I don't know.

Some of the reports I read give me a sense of anger rather than pride. This is true of a lengthy statement made by an Inspector in Keighley who supplied a written reference on my move to traffic. In it he calls me an outstanding officer and prolific thief-taker. He says that I consistently outperformed my colleagues. I am praised as a tutor for my professionalism and enthusiasm. He mentions that he has recommended me three times for Divisional Awards. Talks about me stopping two suicide bids. Goes as far as saying that I am the epitome of what he would want in all his officers. So, you must ask why the feeling of anger. It comes in the following extract:

196

HANDCUFFED EMOTIONS

In my time working with Ben, he has never once let me, his team division, or the organisation down.

So why do I feel let down so badly? That's what I feel anger at. Is that how loyalty and dedication are rewarded in the police force? It's how mine was. Angry as I may be, I also smile at some emails from senior staff. Police speech can be humorous, such as the one I received praising me for my 'hunting' skills in catching thieves. Another for 'fine lock ups.'

When I read the letters and emails from the public, I feel nothing but gratitude. I see them on another level. For someone who has just lost their grandchild in tragic circumstances, to take the time to write and thank you is remarkable.

'On 4th January, my grandson {name withheld} was found in Bradford having died, I presume from hypothermia. Naturally, my daughter, (names withheld} and her partner were devastated. They told me several times how wonderfully kind and considerate your officers were in conveying the news and in all aspects of helping them through a most distressing

experience. I would like to express my gratitude and would ask you to convey these sentiments to the officers involved.'

I always find it so humbling when people who are dealing with traumatic life events that they will probably never fully recover from, want to thank you for doing your job. It's then that I realise, the cliché, just doing your job is a nonsense. Most police officers I know, go above and beyond the line of duty. When I am out there on the front line and I'm holding someone, severely injured in my arms and they are looking up at me, scared and needing help, my humanity takes over. It's more than the carrying out the nuts and bolts of the job, more than being professional and competent. It's about wanting what could be their last moments on Earth to be as compassionate as possible. I think relatives understand that and remember you for it, even if it is for making a good cup of tea.

I should like to take this opportunity to draw your attention to the kindness of thoughtfulness shown to my wife and myself by the two officers who dealt with the death of my son. (name withheld) Particularly P.C. 1965, Ben Pearson who, despite his protestations to the contrary, does make a nice cup of tea. Ben did much to support and comfort us on that sad day and we shall always be grateful to him. You must be very proud to have such men under your command.'

Occasionally, very occasionally, I have received written thanks from a colleague. Now that means something. Every police officer has another police officer's back, that goes without saying, but sometimes a surprise thank you appears out of the blue and makes your day. The one below is such a case.

'Just wanted to say a few words of thanks to Ben and (name withheld) for the other day. Don't know if you are aware of the incident but I had a spill on my push bike in Ilkley whilst on leave. To cut a long story short, I sustained injuries to my head and shoulder which resulted in having clothing cut off me before being placed on a spinal board and taken to hospital by ambulance. This was witnessed by Ben and (name withheld) who assisted in lifting my considerable bulk into the ambulance. One of my main concerns was my bike which is quite an expensive bit of kit and contacting family. Ben and (name withheld) sorted all this out and put my mind at ease. Things are a bit vague regarding what I can remember dur to the dazed state I was in but felt happy knowing they had taken

care of my needs at the time. I'm sure they dealt with me the same they would have any member of the public, but it was comforting that they can also look after 'their own' as well.

I don't know how his family would react to coming second to his bike in terms of concern, but he is right. I treated him as I would treat anyone injured. It's good to know that we were there when one of our own needed us, though. If he ever reads this book. Thanks Pal, I hope the bike recovered from its injuries as you did.

It will have now become clear to anyone reading my book, that I have always taken an immense pride in my driving ability. The final extract commends that ability and I treasure it.

'At 01.35hrs, Tuesday 30th December 2014, West Yorkshire Police were notified of a pursuit travelling along the M62 from GMP area towards Bradford. The subject vehicle an Audi A7 (reg withheld). Due to speeds of 130 mph the vehicle evaded GMB officers. A few moments later the vehicle was sighted by PC's (name withheld) and Ben Pearson who were in a marked police vehicle together on the M606 heading towards Bradford at speeds over 100 mph.

HANDCUFFED EMOTIONS

The officers began to follow the vehicle and again the vehicle failed to stop, accelerating away from the officers towards Bradford City Centre. PC Pearson was the driver and PC (name withheld) commenced a commentary requesting TPAC authority and updating on the current location and risk associated with the subject vehicle. The pursuit was authorised, and I continued to listen to the pursuit and periodically viewed the pursuit via the CCTV in the Force Command Hub. The subject vehicle eventually crashed, and the two occupants were arrested.

As a previous Roads Policing Inspector, Head of Driver Training, and a member of the National Strategic Pursuit Group I can say this pursuit and commentary is one of the best I have heard. The FCH were constantly updated in a clear and concise manner and the driving was undertaken in a professional manner with no risk to members of the public. I thank both officers for their professionalism in this pursuit and only wish others could match the standards displayed.'

I know my mental health is fractured, which is perhaps why these 'thank you' letters mean so much to me. I wonder if when they were being written, the people I helped would ever know that they would now become part of my healing process? I'm proud of every award I have received. I'm proud of the bravery and tenacity I showed dealing with the most dangerous offenders. Yes, all officers go out to just do their job, but recognition of it is like the icing on the cake. It makes the sacrifices worthwhile.

Going Code 11

To sit and ask yourself a direct question that you know needs an answer, otherwise you must question, what is the point of it all? What has this been about, is hard? The question I ask myself is what have I learned? Am I going to come out of this better than I went in? I know I'm a weaker person now; I feel that every day. I'm not as strong as I thought I was. I wonder how many 44-year-olds come to a point in their life where they stand back and look at what they have learned? I thought that was something you did in your old age. To me, I must know that my illness has taught me important life lessons. I must justify what has happened to me. The importance of being able to answer such questions is a big part of my recovery.

I accept what I have seen and had to do is not normal. I had a goal for how many years I would achieve as an officer. I'm disappointed that I have not reached that goal, but I have realised that I need not do 30 years to say I've done well. I'm happy at what I've achieved. I know my career as a police officer has gone but If I weren't poorly, I wouldn't be able to hold my hands up and say that. One of the real lessons I have learned is that nothing is set in concrete, there is no such thing as permanent. We can't say what will happen tomorrow, we can only hope we have the understanding to deal with it.

I've stereotyped many people in my life, blanked a lot because of the job I do, and avoided speaking to others. I have made wrong decisions and choices because of my job, but I realise now that it is only a job. Yes, it's given me fulfilment and led me down a good pathway but coming to understand that just because you do something at work, it doesn't have to be the be all and end all.

To realise that as I am authoring this book about my career, someone could ring me up and tell me it's all over for me. They have made the decision to pension me off because of C-PTSD. My immediate thought on that would be that I have given them everything I could give. If someone stayed at my home for a while, I wouldn't expect them to obey every order I laid down, yet that is what I have done for 19 years. I've been controlled by an organisation. I've been a puppet; I felt that. Any police officer knows, irrespective of what team they are in, they have invested totally in their roles. To the higher ups, though, I feel we are like pawns to be juggled wherever we can be best used.

If there is a Millwall game on for example, even though they know about it for a long time, at the last minute, they will cancel your rest days. A common event, but you must do as you are told. It's a bubble and you are in it being tossed about until it pops. For me, it popped when they diagnosed my illness. It was now causing stress, and that isn't acceptable. I disrupted the order of things, so I am no longer wanted. What have I learned from that? A lot, I am not indispensable or indestructible. I have a frailty like all human beings, and I am not ashamed to say that. As a police officer, I would have been. I no longer must be the hard guy, and it's a good feeling.

The police saw what I was good at and they have let me be that cop and do my best. I have had some great times, some of the best lock ups. I worked with the best teams. I will never regret what I've done. I've put people away for years. Seen them given life sentences and every one of them deserved it. I've done my fair share for the community, but I know now that when it's done, it's done. I am just a name and a number. PC 1965, Ben Pearson.

If I have any regrets, it would be that I didn't show my parents how much I loved them or travelled as much as I would have liked. I was always busy catching thieves, pursuing stolen vehicles and working silly hours. I should have put the demons to bed years ago, and I never did. There was stuff I should have put to rest, but I know I wear my heart on my sleeve and sometimes that has worked against me. I've often held things close I should have talked about.

Now, I'm not afraid to talk out anymore. I understand increasingly how important it is to express yourself. When I first joined the force, I was told to act like a sponge, take everything in and accept it. Soak it up and make a name for yourself. Once you make a name for yourself doors will open. If you make a shit name for yourself, choose how hard you try. Those doors will remain closed. I made a good name for myself. Before I became ill, I know I could have gone to most offices in the police, especially in the Ops Units. I know the more you are known as a prolific thief-taker and diligent officer; the more door opens.

I now look back and I know I spent too much time with my head down working and not enough time chatting to people. I took on a lot of things that I just don't think I should have taken on. I never realised how much you could learn from others by sitting down and listening to them. I always wanted to crack on. I never took a break for myself. I should have sat more with the lads and I didn't. Taking some time for me never came into my head. I can admit now that I put myself on a pedestal and I wanted to keep myself there, so I worked hard to do that. Remember; I didn't know how my health would be affected by it.

Even when days were shit and nothing was happening. Like when the World Cup was on and there were no cars on the road, no people walking, no logs coming in. It was like there had been an apocalypse. It felt like I was the only police car on the road with nowhere to go. I would wind myself up then because I wasn't coming back with arrests when I knew there was crime out there, but I couldn't do anything about it. I pushed myself to the limits. I know that, and I have suffered for that. I have burnt myself out for the sake of what?

Why did I always do that? It came from my dad who used to say to me. 'Work hard if you want to get anywhere.' I have always had that in mind. The more effort I put in, the more I will get back. If you don't try, then you won't get sod all in life. To give 100% to all I do is the way I am made. If they based promotion on the quality and amount of work you did, then I would have made inspector years ago. It's not, it's based on exams, and being dyslexic, I'm not good at that. Had it been about the arrests, the extra work, the effort put in, the personal sacrifices made and the growth as a police officer, I think I would be a promoted officer well before now.

Has my dyslexia held me back? A question I ask myself often. I think I would have to say to you that fear has held me back. I know I can speak to anyone, whether it be Gary Barlow or the Prime Minister with no worry at all, but fear of failure with exams, standing in front of a board and writing out four reasons for social diversity, scares me. Is that related to my dyslexia, probably? As it stopped me earning stripes, yes it has.

I once went in for the position of force negotiator because I knew I was good at talking to people. I was told I couldn't move forward because I hadn't got a stripe on my shoulder. I had to be a ranking officer to speak to a Chief Constable, to project myself. Well, hold on there. Does a stripe suddenly make me a different person? Does it change my abilities, abilities which I have proven over and over? I didn't go to college; I didn't get a degree, but I went to the school of hard knocks and I succeeded.

When it gets to Corporate, I understand they are looking for different people. They want politicians at that level and there seems to be a belief that university graduates are more capable than the rest. At sergeant level, skill is important, so I don't think that's true, but above that they are seeking businessmen, stroke politicians. I don't remember the last time I saw a member of the SLT (senior leadership team) going out in a police car, arresting people. They are always at meetings, pulling figures, looking at budgets. Who can we put there, what do we do with this? Don't misunderstand me here, I know that is necessary, but I think the danger comes when they get too detached from the reality of the job.

There are some fantastic superintendents, I know a couple, but they are the ones who keep their fingers on the pulse. Yes, they must be Corporate with things, but they also must have a clue about what's out there, what's going on at night. How many cars are covering any one area at a time? I don't think some of them have any idea about that. If I were to say one lesson that Corporate officers could learn it would be, 'spend some time on the street as part of your ongoing training.'

Since being diagnosed with C-PTSD I have learned a lot about Mental Health. I only hope those in command have learned the same. There is a lot of talk about mental health issues now, and people are being asked to come forward and speak about their problems. We see film stars, medical professionals, and even royalty talking about the suffering they go through. We don't see the police force coming forward to talk about it.

From day one in the police the chances are, you are going to get assaulted, run down, killed, or get PTSD. As soon as you get out on the Motorway Unit you are told to put your high vis on because you could get run down. Wear your stab vest because you could get shot or stabbed. They drill it into you, always put your high vis on when attending a road traffic collision. It's all about protecting your body physically, but what about protecting what's going on in your mind? Zilch, blank, there is nothing said.

HANDCUFFED EMOTIONS

As I have said before, there are posters in the police station, one shows a woman crying saying I want my son back. So, you are asking, 'well, where has her son gone?' He's there, but he's not there. They aim the messages to anyone coming into the station. There is also a notice on the back of the toilet door. It reads. '84% of men between 38 and 48 commit suicide because of circumstances....... Talk, hashtag. Mental health.' But you can't talk, you can't bring it up to anyone. They are saying the right things, but they don't expect you to act on it. As soon as you do they pigeonhole you. I have learned that the hard way.

It's time now for the police force to stand up and be counted. To take more positive action in addressing mental health. They now have a system where you can report a police officer for doing wrong things and its anonymous. Why can't they have an anonymous line for mental health? Why can't I leave a message saying, 'look, I'm struggling here?' Or have an anonymous forum where someone from Occy Health or a nurse or a doctor picks it up and sends it back with recommendations that are helpful? 'Here's a number, call us now on this number confidentially.' A line that's monitored 24 a day. Surely, they owe us that much? They must be realistic about the number of bobbies who are buckling and have nowhere to go.

I set my twitter up to do that. To just tell people how I am feeling and listen to them in return. It is letting people know they can talk. This could be a life where someone is ready to swing from a tree or a bannister. Prisoners are treated better. If a prisoner comes in with a cut or a bruise or suspected of being mentally unwell, we take immediate action to protect that person. There are extensive guidelines in the Police Policies and Procedures Handbook. One-part states: *When a person is detained under the MHA, police have legal responsibility to take to a place of safety.* I snap at an incident and I'm sent to do my report.

In the Management of Health & Safety at Work Regulations (1999) Under the Health & Safety Principals, step 4 says: *Running initiatives to raise awareness of health issues at work, when appropriate, and signposting employees to advice on health and wellbeing.* It sounds good and well, but unless employees are assured that to talk is okay, they never will.

HANDCUFFED EMOTIONS

In the paper, 'Responding to Trauma in Policing' Chief Constable Andy Rhodes who is the National Head for Wellbeing & Engagement wrote in the foreword: *We need to do much more if we are to instil the confidence in our people we care deeply about their mental health.* He also talked about the importance of people needing to feel confident to say' I'm not okay' without being judged a failure. A challenge he saw in 'blue light' cultures.

I see the changes now taking place as being too late for me, but I hope that the lessons learned mean no one else suffers in the same way. I don't know, talk is so easy, saying the right things are easy, but taking the correct action needs resilience and commitment. I would like to see a national initiative called 'It's all right to talk.' One that is meant and recognised as being needed now. Not in some distant future, but NOW. I would like to see dedicated psychiatrists or qualified therapists present in the workplace to offer help and guidance before it gets too late. The present process of waiting for an appointment for Occy Health, then seeing a nurse who refers you to a doctor, takes weeks and weeks. A prisoner would be referred to someone straight away or taken to hospital.

BENJAMIN PEARSON

I have been away from work for nearly a year now. During that time, my own Sergeant has been absent with different issues but keeps in touch with mutual support by emails and texts. Not one other senior person has contacted me to ask about my wellbeing, how I am coping or is there anything they can do. NO ONE!

Important to me now is not how fast or for how many miles I can drive. Who is in front of me, or behind me? Simplicity has become the key to my recovery. The less I think about, the better. When we go out now, Milly drives, she plans the journey and where we are going. Our roles have switched, but it's the only way I can cope. Now when I drive, I've become one of those people who piss people off for driving slowly. My mind can't cope with too many stimuli. I must process things differently. But that's okay. The need I had to be at the top of my game brought me here. I couldn't relax my thoughts; The traumatic events played over and over in my mind. Now I know I don't have to do that, and I realise I must block such memories out to get well again. I never did that before.

HANDCUFFED EMOTIONS

Changes have had to be made. My reliance, as most people, on mobile phones, for example. At one time, if I lost my mobile, I would have been horrified. My day evolved around being in contact, available always. If I lost my phone today, so what? It's not the end of the world. The action that I always craved doesn't matter anymore. It's burnt me out emotionally and physically and for what? I recall once cutting grass when I was a greenkeeper at Northcliffe. There was dew on the grass, and the gangs on the mower made beautiful stripes. A rainbow was in the sky. The fairways looked stunning. You can't get better than that. I'd love to go back to that tractor and sit in the mist and look over the hills.

I was always looking for something better. I didn't appreciate there was nothing better than the silence of a peaceful morning. To me, I thought I deserved more. I wanted more; my goals became different; they drove me to achieve. To become a law enforcer, Ben, a man to be reckoned with. When I think back, the strangest thing is that me and my oppo used to go up to Baildon Moor when out on patrol. We used to take photos of the sunset. It was a highlight of our week. We felt privileged to do that. How many people sit and watch the

215

sun come up? See the snow fresh on the tops? A mist over the valley? Circumstances may be different, but I will do that again. I want to sit there with Milly and feel the same sense of beauty. No more, no less.

Above the Horizon

What's next for me, for my family, I can only guess. I know they are trying to retire me now, I'm 44 years old and I have 19 years of police experience, but I've got an empty page in my book. Where do I go? What do I do? Will I ever be well again? All what's and ifs. I was thinking the other day that I now have an empty book with no title, bits, and bats of experience in it, but no direction. It's the best way I can explain it. I can write anything I want to in it and I have a lot of skills, but nothing knows where it wants to be. That may sound confusing to someone reading this, but if they are suffering in the way I am, they will know exactly what I mean.

What I know for certain is that my health will always come first now, along with my family. They are the permanents in my life, all else means little in comparison. Before I would have looked for a job to get x, y, z. I don't care now what job I do as long as I get a fair day's pay for a hard day's work. I'm not too proud to take on any job as long as it gives me what I need to support my family. Before I can really move forward with any ideas I have, I must wake up from this nightmare I am in.

I talk about this with Milly and she will tell me that whatever happens it must be better than the last few years. She sees writing this book as an important part of my therapy. I know people will read this and come to different conclusions. Some will totally understand the difficulties I've written about. Others will lack the understanding. It doesn't really matter. Mental health isn't a straightforward issue, it comes in many guises with many outcomes. No one knows, until it hits them, what it's going to mean for them. I'm no different. Milly knows that.

We talk openly about the people who have shielded away from me, and those who have supported me. We take each day as it comes, nothing is certain in life and it owes no one anything. Shit happens and we must move forward. I do that slowly and I have her full support. I laugh when she turns to me and says, 'you're stuck with me for life.' I kind of think it's the other way around.

What really matters to me is when Milly tells me she is proud of me for putting myself on the line. For making people aware of what goes on in the mind of someone suffering from C-PTSD. Opening myself up to criticisms I may get from others is a small price to pay if I help others in the same situation. I hope, one day, to write a follow-up book about my life after the police force featuring the recovered, mentally well, Ben Pearson. For now, I'm satisfied to raise awareness. PTSD can affect anyone. Speaking out is important.

Milly has told me she sees her job differently now. It has changed massively. Her love of being a front-line officer has gone for fear she will end up like me. She's seen limbs hanging off people, children dead, and had to deal with the insurmountable grief of parents. Her decision to come off the front line pleases me. I am now less fearful for her. Her reasons amaze me. She doesn't want to have to come home and tell me about some horrific incident because of the impact on me.

Taking the role of a TriM practitioner is important to her because she has witnessed the suffering I have gone through, and still am going through. She is pleased the police have now implemented a support system. Milly will say that I never received such support. It wasn't available to me. Would the outcome have been different? Who knows, we both think so. The future for her is one of concern for me. She worries I will see myself as a failure, someone who has let people down. The kudos that being a police officer has in society she knows I will no longer warrant any more.

Those kids who see me on Police Interceptors and run to get my autograph because they look up to me. How will I be affected when I'm no longer a police officer on a TV show? It scares Milly that people know me only in one role and recognise me in the street as Ben the policeman on telly. Once back in civvy street it will become an enormous challenge. Mentally, when you have been in one job a long time, you think differently in situations. You are more aware of what is around you. You don't sit in a pub with your back to people; you are aware of risk. You look at people and think, 'they are behaving strangely.' The fear I won't adapt to a new life, and one in which Milly becomes the primary worker, will be a major shift in our roles and is always present. We both know it will be hard, but to survive we must cope with it.

What I would want to do now, job wise, is something I'll be happy in. I'd like to sell motorbikes again or work with my brother like old times. I'd like to travel and do stuff I have never done, but nothing police related. I'd like to do things that help other people with what I've learned, whether that be talking about PTSD, talking about mental health. It doesn't matter. I'm not a trained counsellor or anything like that, but all I want to do is to turn around and say. 'This is what I went through, therefore I struggle, and this is what I didn't do and it's what I think people should be doing.' It's important to me because there is a massive gap there. Unless you have been through it or done it. It's alright sitting on the outside but unless you have been there you cannot know the reality.

You can give someone all the directions in the world about what happened in a plane crash, but unless you have been in that crash, and it's hit the floor and you have felt that intense fear, you do not understand. You cannot feel the fear or the pain at that moment of impact. I want to let them see that. I've opened my twitter page and made it acceptable to talk about mental health. I've been contacted by different agencies and they have asked me to speak on radio. I don't know if I want to do that but, in the long run, but I would like to think I have done something from all of this to help people. What do I say when I get young officers coming up to me and asking, 'Am I doing the right thing?' I point out that I am one in thousands and If they want to do it, they should. Just be aware of what can happen, be aware of the signs. Know what to look for, I didn't.

I can tell you all the things I'd like to do. I'd like to be in security where I can go to people's houses and explain to them how to keep their home safe. Where the weak spots are on their home so they can protect themselves. I'd like to make them aware of the bad people out there who are just waiting to take advantage of the good people. My illness stops me from doing certain things, however. I just can't think that far ahead. I can see myself going back to the man I was without the blue cubes. The Ben who had a massive positive outlook on life. I want to say to people that no matter how shitty it gets, there is always an end view.

HANDCUFFED EMOTIONS

I won't let my illness define who I am or make me less of a person than I am. It's an illness, people have many illnesses. I can recover. I remember when Aids was first spoken about; it was like a death sentence. Today its curable and the stigma has gone from it. C-PTSD is an illness. It pushes me down, and it knocks me back, but I know I must turn around and tell myself it's part of my journey in life. I'm not in a dress rehearsal. This is it. If it beats me, the only person who has allowed that is me. Life will not stop for me. I can sit and mope about it or I can get on it, push it and ride with it.

I send positive quotes to people every day. I use to think I could only do that if I wore a uniform and drove a car. I now know I don't. I can be nice to people and show them I care. I try now to identify if people have boxes and don't know how to cope. The messages I get on twitter say it all. People need understanding. Don't pretend to listen to them but look elsewhere when they talk. Be interested and help. If I had a friend who was drowning in a swimming pool, I'd get them out. Anybody would, so why not help that same friend if they have mental health issues? It's not contagious, it doesn't spread.

223

My twitter groups are all about helping where there is a mental health need. It's also a positive thing for me. When I put something out and get something back, it helps me. What most don't realise is that when you are in your four walls you are alone; your mind can play many tricks and does. Conversing on twitter means you are not alone. There are many people stuck in four walls suffering from serious mental illness, twitter is a way to relieve their isolation. They know I'm there for them and I know they are there for me. When I get back replies thanking me for my messages, its heart-warming and really boosts me. I'm no one special but I've been there, seen it and understand it.

I'm positive about the future with Milly and the kids now. We have spent more time together than ever before. I know that's because I haven't been working, but it's still been a grand thing. Once she changes her role, I won't have the worry of her on the beat. She won't be in a vulnerable position; her hours will change, and we will have more time as a family. For me personally, I will now be able to see more things through the eyes of my children. Things like Halloween, Christmas plays, school open days. We can all go as a family; we haven't been able to do that before.

HANDCUFFED EMOTIONS

I want to have that feeling I used to have when I watch them play. That spark which I've lost. I don't feel now, but I know I will get it back. I can feel that things are changing. There are little bits of light coming through now. I will push nothing. If it takes another 12 months or two years, so be it. I can see above the horizon now. I go out and feel the sunshine on my face and look at what is around me. I stopped doing that before. I saw nothing. I was so closed in. Now I am feeling some enjoyment coming back. Little sparks inside. I've appreciated things more.

Yes, my life is different to everyone else's, but it's still okay. I may be ill, but I know I still have a family that loves me, and I love them. My brother is still there for me. I can talk to him openly about my illness and he understands. Hopes and dreams still exist and there are things I want to do, and I know once I am out of the police I will focus on my future and the things I want. It may not be the same future I saw for myself before, but it will be a good one. The shackles holding me in the police force will be broken and I will feel some freedom to be the old Ben again.

BENJAMIN PEARSON

When I look at the pattern, my day takes now, it reminds me of Christmas and holiday time. Days merge and have no real meaning. I have no direction in my life; I try to keep a structure if I can for the kids. I try to split my day into three parts. Morning is for doing tasks, afternoon is play with my children, maybe a walk, the park, or a game at home. Evening is family relaxation time; we may go down to the pub for tea or just settle down. To some people they may feel I have it easy, but it's far from the truth. I want a job; I want to feel useful to society again. It's important to me to come out of all of this and lead a fulfilling life where I'm not scared of sleeping for fear of my nightmares. A life where I get up in the morning, refreshed after a good night's sleep, ready for a hard day's work.

I flip a lot of ideas around in my head. Acting is something I could look at; I am familiar with how television works. I would enjoy doing that, but for the first couple of months after I am no longer in the force, I will wing it. See what happens, get well. I would like to think I will then be able to look at my opportunities. What I won't be doing any more is over planning as I have had to in the police. I see Milly in that situation now. Everything must be precise, thought out, timed. I was like that. Now, I ask myself, does it really matter? She enjoys that because I have taken a lot of pressure from her by being at home and doing the things Milly would probably have done before.

As I look back over my 19 years as a police officer with too many assaults to remember. I see my arms covered with scars. I have been head-butted, attacked with knives, hammers, bricks, razors. Cars I've been driving rammed. On one occasion, as mentioned previously, I suffered a concussion from an impact that landed me in hospital with a head injury. My brain was bruise affecting my speech and memory. It took years of treatment and speech therapy to cure the stutter it left me with.

I also remember vividly the time someone ran me down and broke my arm. To this day, my knees remain damaged, and my hips are displaced. The list goes on and on. I have witnessed women kicking the hell out of men, men slapping women, drunks just fighting anybody in their path. Listened as bystanders' egg them on, been spat on, abused, and called every name under the sun. The sadness is, this is the norm, it is what a police officer expects to face every day on the job.

Every day brings another challenge. Another dangerous situation.

Besides the injuries, attacks and insults I have faced. Along with my teammates, I have missed birthdays, Christmases, weddings, holidays. Sat holding the hands of dying victims trapped in road traffic collisions. Given CPR to over 20 people, most of which didn't survive, all the while appearing to remain the stoic copper just doing his job.

I want to put all of that behind me now. I want the nightmares to stop and the fear I feel at the sound of a siren, to go away. Above all, I want this book to reach out to others in my situation; I want them to feel someone cares. They matter, their lives matter. I want the book to be of benefit to anyone who has mental illness. Accept what has happened to them but recognise it doesn't mean it's the end for them. I admire anyone who has the courage to come forth and tell their story. I didn't think I had it in me to do this but, hard as it has been, I have done it. The more people who speak out, stand up and be counted, the more organisations will realise their responsibilities and make the changes needed to protect people like me.

HANDCUFFED EMOTIONS

Where do my thoughts rest now? Do I have deep regrets? No! My experiences have made me the person I am today. Take away the PTSD and illness and it has made me the dad I am and partner to Milly. I wouldn't be a role model to friends and neighbours and have the respect I have from those I have helped. For every hurtful memory there is a good time, a heart-warming time. Seeing officers, I have tutored grow to become exceptional officers, seeing children sat in my car wearing my hat with pride. Memories such as these make my heart glow warmly and no illness is going to take that away from me. Will I know when I am well again. I want to relay one more story to answer that. It may seem strange to conclude my book with a story, but it embodies all that I was, and all that I am, and will be again.

The story begins at Christmas, I would have been around 12 years of age. The lights on the tree twinkled, and it filled me with excitement. Mum was playing her favourite festive tape on a cassette. Shaking Stevens, John Lennon, Mud. All the old classics. She was cooking in the kitchen and the house smelled of stuffing and turkey. Laughter was everywhere and the pure joy of the season hung in the air. It's hard to explain the feeling of warmth and love that existed. A feeling that stayed with me and grew deeper, year on year. Christmas became such a special time to me. It meant family. Even when mum and dad moved to Spain, the feeling remained, strong as it had ever been. No matter where I was or what I did.

There was one time when I woke up one Christmas morning, during police training days, to find myself alone in an Ibis Hotel because I had nowhere else to stay. My clothes were in bin bags. The only possession I owned was my bright yellow Renault Mégane Coupe. Alone, feeling flat. I had cheese and ham sandwiches for my Christmas dinner, swilled down with a few cans of Carling. I fell asleep and woke up again at around 3am, cold and shivering, I dragged myself into bed, but as I lay there it still filled my heart with that same child's joy. I lay and thought of those cheap tree lights we had with the spikey glass covers. I smiled at the memory of dad standing on them on the floor and swearing. Christmas was Christmas, no matter where I was.

Then it all changed. I can't remember when, but I noticed the feeling had disappeared. I felt that all the magic had been placed in a jar with the lid screwed on tightly and placed in a dark cellar deep within me. From that moment it didn't matter what took place at Christmas, the jam jar remained firmly shut. I knew it was there. It was visible to me each time I looked inside of myself. I could see the memories, lights and smells but failed to feel the joy. I resigned myself to never experiencing that happiness again. I saw myself as odd, grown up, but without feeling. I didn't even feel a buzz from my children's eyes as they woke up on Christmas mornings. I feel extremely saddened, but try as I may, I can't open the jam jar that traps my Christmas spirit within it.

So, to answer the question, when will I know I am well again? It will be when I share the joy in my children's faces, feel the magical moment they look in amazement at their presents. It will be when the memories of my boyhood happiness and the love I felt at Christmas are released. Or when my eyes sparkle with expectation as I put the lights on the tree and watch two little faces light up with them. Then I will know. Until that moment, it's alright to be different. To be ill. It's okay not to be okay.

BENJAMIN PEARSON

Meet the Author

Ben Pearson has spent the last 19 years of his life fighting crime. He is in the elite Roads Policing Unit of West Yorkshire Police, featured in the hit TV series "Police Interceptors" showing on Channel 5. As a decorated officer, he has driven in the fastest, most dangerous pursuits. Arrested murders, rapists, alongside high-profile burglars. Taken down the most violent of offenders, bringing them to justice. Unbeknown to

HANDCUFFED EMOTIONS

Ben, his greatest fight was yet to come. After dealing with a series of heinous, fatal collisions and losing his parents, Ben's mind became his worst enemy. '**Handcuffed Emotions – A Police Interceptor's Drive into Darkness'**, tells of his fight, not only for his family, his health, and his sanity, but against a System that failed him.

Ben's journey stretches from his early training days as a recruit, through the reality of life as a police officer and known TV personality into the dark depths of **PTSD**. The incidents are real. His emotions overwhelming. The illness devastating. His remarkable handling of it courageous. Handcuffed Emotions is a must read for anyone who had suffered debilitating traumas and faced mental illness. It is both enlightening, thought provoking and brings hope to those who suffer in silence.

BENJAMIN PEARSON

POSTSCRIPT:

Since this book has been written Ben Pearson has now left the police force on medical grounds. He now champions mental illness awareness, and as such, 20% of profits from his memoir are being donated to:

The Kaleidoscope Plus Group

Kaleidoscope Plus is a leading mental health charity, founded in 1973. It supports and assists anyone who has a mental illness and needs help and support by delivering valuable services to communities across the UK. The group has a free, confidential text line at Text Team KPG to 85258 plus a national helpline.

National telephone help line 08000590123

www.kaleidoscope.org.uk

Donations to Kaleidoscope:

Mental health issues are on the rise in the UK and need support. Inadequate funding makes this difficult so please donate to: TEXT BENP 3 to 70085 to donate £3

Printed in Great Britain
by Amazon